Let This Mind Be In You

Let This Mind Be In You

The Quest for Identity
through Oedipus to Christ

SEBASTIAN MOORE

Darton, Longman and Todd
London

First published 1985 by
Darton, Longman and Todd Ltd
89 Lillie Road, London SW6 1UD

© 1985 Sebastian Moore

ISBN 0 232 51644 8

British Library Cataloguing in Publication Data

Moore, Sebastian
  Let this mind be in you.
  1. Jesus Christ
  I. Title
  232   BT202

  ISBN 0–232–51644–8

Phototypeset by Input Typesetting Ltd, London SW19 8DR
Printed and bound in Great Britain by
Anchor Brendon Ltd, Tiptree, Essex

To
Matt Lamb

Let this mind be in you
   which also was in Christ Jesus.

Though he was in the form of God,
   he did not deem equality with God
   something to be grasped at.
Rather, he emptied himself
   and took the form of a slave,
   being born in the likeness of humankind.

He was known to be of human estate,
   and it was thus that he humbled himself,
   obediently accepting even death,
   death on a cross.

Because of this,
   God highly exalted him
   and bestowed on him the name
   above every other name,

So that at Jesus' name
   every knee must bend
   in the heavens, on the earth,
   and under the earth,
   and every tongue proclaim
   to the glory of God the Father:
   JESUS CHRIST IS LORD!

(Philippians 2:5–11)

Contents

vii

viii

Conclusion: Let This Mind Be in You   123

Preface

This book, I hope, is about you. It is certainly about me. I am trying to point to, to name, to describe, and to understand that centre in each of us where both hope and despair, both faith and doubt, both love and indifference, are born.

There is only one centre, only one you, one I. There is not, I mean, one source of good, another of evil attitudes and deeds. One identical, highly elusive feeling and felt self hungers for an unimaginable fullness of life and plunges impatiently and desperately, or inclines through boredom, to evil. The same *feeling* goes both ways.

Thus to explore the feeling as it awakes to fuller life is our indispensable preparation for understanding our propensity to take the other way; and this not by contrasting it with the good way not taken but rather by awakening to a sense of the self in its essential ambivalence, a wobble, a wonkiness, that is at once what a sinful inertia exploits and a skilful grace captivates. That is the sense of self that this book seeks to awaken.

So I start by reflecting on this centre in its awakening to fuller life. At heart, I sense that I am desirable, and this sense is awakened whenever I am attracted to another and, because and only because thus awakened, I want to be desired by that other. This is the theme of my first quadrant.

As well as, and in contrast with, this awakening of the sense of being desirable through attraction to another, thus indirectly, there is an experience of being directly awakened to my desirableness by the mysterious reality whose desiring *makes* me desirable. This is the theme of my second quadrant.

Thus I reach three axioms, which are the backbone of this book. We only live by desire. We only desire out of a sense of being desirable. We only feel desirable absolutely because we are absolutely desired.

xi

In the third quadrant, I set this basic grammar of desire in its full anthropological and historical context, where for the first time the essential ambivalence of our centre appears. The feeling and felt self comes to be out of a drama, first of psychological separation from the mother, then of a more complex, triangulated interaction with mother and father, these dramas being but the reverberation of an original drama, of the birth of self-awareness in the immemorially evolving animal. It is the fragile, vulnerable, society-dependent birth of self-awareness that gives it its essential ambivalence. And it is this initial dependence of our self-awareness on the socio-drama in which it is first formed that is the reason why we 'cling to that dimension' and resist the impulse of the spirit to become who we truly are, the desired of God, the Christ. This profound resistance to growth is original or generic sin. The whole human race is in a condition of arrested development.

In the fourth quadrant, I try to understand how Jesus liberates us from this self-imposed captivity. Free of it himself, he freed his followers. How he did so is to be understood by applying the principle of indirect and direct awakening of the sense of being desirable, elaborated in quadrants one and two respectively. Jesus awoke his followers to the maximum possible within the limits of indirect, social arousal. They had the only experience there has ever been of the limit of this life *in* this life. With this life's possibility for liberation through indirect arousal exhausted, there remained only the *direct* arousal, which they experienced as *Jesus in their midst*. The movement of the heart, in which God is directly known, finds its focus in the person in their midst. The socializing of the deepest human privacy is the appearing of God in the flesh. The risen Jesus is the moment of the incarnation. The gospel becomes ecstatically explicit when Thomas cries out to the wounded one, 'My Lord and my God!'

With this breakthrough, the Holy Spirit is that experience of being created that is the new creation, and the original power – that an immemorial dialectic of sin and disaster has rendered darkly problematic – shows itself to the heart as the loving one, the Abba of Jesus.

In a concluding section, I move beyond the passion, death and resurrection as experienced by the disciples, as lived through by them, to consider the intention of Jesus himself, that 'mind' in which he embraced a wretched and horrible death. I have not attempted this transition before. It is only now that I have attempted it that I see how seriously incomplete is a salvation theology without it. This section gives me the title for the present work.

Finally, I have decided, with some encouragement, to include the notes taken during a recent directed retreat. There are two reasons why I thought this might be helpful. First, it emerged with startling clarity during the retreat that the attitude to Jesus crucified that I had enjoined in *The Crucifed Jesus is No Stranger* was one I had not appropriated emotionally myself: that of bringing into direct imaginative contact my own resistant self and the pierced man on the cross. Thus *The Crucified*, for all its rhetoric, was at its nerve centre still in the head. The vision there presented still needed enfleshment. The second reason has to do with why I had not been able to make this emotional rapprochement with the crucified. I had not understood that my *resistance* to the healing comes *from* the heart, from that 'wobble' which is I. I had *said* that each of us is at once crucifier and crucified, but I had not been able to mean it.

The reason I had not been able to mean it is a weakness which the whole Christian tradition suffers, and must recover from if it is to heal our desperate time. We haven't got to 'the wobble' in ourselves that is psychologically *prior* to sinfulness, where we are indistinguishably sinned against and sinning. Thus the deepest diagnosis the tradition offers is moral and thus symptom-centred. We don't touch the pre-moral nerve where saints and monsters take their rise, and which the pierced heart of God touches and totally transforms, the pierced heart that with love's final aggressiveness says to the beloved, 'I *am* you!'

There is no area of Christian action, from prayer and spiritual direction to political and liberation theology, that is not kept from finding a focus by this unawareness of the pre-moral core of our being. The critique of 'sinful social structures' will fail until we learn emotionally to make our own the one heart that is the creative victim of these heartless empires.

Finally I want to honour a wonderful friend. Tony Palese has worked with me these ten years or more. A born archivist, he has kept my work in order, a task hopelessly beyond the psyche to which the reader is about to be exposed. An unrelenting encourager, he got me to take time off for this book, and worked with me on it for long hours while I stayed with him and Chris his wife. I love them both – and there are so many others of the Marquette community. May the Spirit draw our wobbling hearts into a community of love.

Birthday of John the Baptist, 1984   SEBASTIAN MOORE

Acknowledgements

All the scriptural quotations are taken from the New American Bible.

The poems in this book are the author's own unless otherwise stated.

The quotations from 'Four Quartets' and 'The Waste Land' are reprinted by permission of Faber and Faber Ltd and Harcourt Brace Jovanovich Inc from *Collected Poems 1909–1962* by T. S. Eliot. The quotation from 'The Tower beyond Tragedy' is reprinted from *The Selected Poetry of Robinson Jeffers* by permission of Random House Inc. The translation from Dante's *Divine Comedy* is by John Ciardi, published by Mentor Books, New American Library Inc.

1.

Overview

1 Underlying desire is the sense that *I am desirable*. This sense is intensified by my desiring another, and more so by my being desired by that other, which brings me into intimacy. In all this, and in all interhuman relating, I feel my desirability *indirectly*.	**3** My origin (and the race's origin as evolving from animal) involves *separation* from the 'glory' of symbiosis, hence a *diminutation of the sense of being desirable*, and consequent complexification of relationships, male–female and others. There is a 'withdrawal of God', the falling of a shadow across the sunlit garden of our infancy. The shadow is not evil. It is the climate in which evil grows. 'Original sin'.
2 There is also a *direct* experience of my desirableness, not through desiring an object but from within. Thus awakened to myself, I desire I know not what. This is a yearning for *intimacy with that which, by desiring me, makes me to be, to be desirable*: God.	**4** The recovery of glory. Jesus, a new humanity *free from the curse of reduced sense of our goodness and of God*, communicates this 'contagion' to his disciples. He communicates this new sense of human desirability to the maximum possible within the limits of indirect, inter-human arousal (1). This new life of the disciples collapses with his death. After his death, they experience him as *directly* arousing their sense of their goodness, i.e. as God. The 'glorified' Jesus, restoring the early 'glory' (3), and the new life (Holy Spirit).

The First Quadrant

2.

Establishing a grammar of desire

The two basic facts about us are that we notice things and that we want things. These two facts, of attention and desire, are becoming very apparent in the life of the infant. Now attention is *to* something. And if you reflect, you will see that this attention is *to something already going on in and around yourself*, a response to your surroundings, which attention sharpens. And this hitherto unnoticed response is part of a continuous state of self-awareness, of the self aware without particular attention.

Now it must be the same with the other basic activity, of wanting things. Wanting this or that cannot possibly be the start of the wanting process. It too must be preceded by a continuous condition of myself in my environment, a continuous wanting-I-know-not what, a 'just wanting'.

Now what is this 'just wanting' state? If we don't reflect carefully, at this point, on our experience, we will say, 'It is a state of emptiness wanting to be filled'. But if we reflect, we see that this is the opposite of the truth. 'Just wanting' is a feeling good that wants to go on feeling good and looks for things to feel good about. This is very clear in the child. The child – like the dolphin – is a bundle of pleasurableness. Freud describes our original condition, moving in the amniotic fluid, as the 'oceanic' condition.

Thus as we move, in our inquiry, from the definite, specific wants, back to the undifferentiated 'just wanting', we are moving towards *not emptiness but fullness*. In the life of desire, it is 'everything' that becomes 'this thing'; it is not 'nothing' that becomes 'this thing'.

Thus every specific wishing is an intensification of feeling good, just as every act of attention is a focusing of the self aware. And because a specific wish intensifies my feeling good, a wish whose object is another person is especially promising for me: for in this case my feeling good, which is *awakened* in desiring, may perhaps

5

be *exercised* in my being desired by the other person. *Feeling* good, I seek to *be* good for someone else.

Thus the basic grammar of human relating is laid down. A person who awakens my desire makes me feel good. I want this good feeling to be fully exercised in my being desired by that person. I look to the cause of my desire for the exercising of the good self-feeling in which my desire is grounded.

I put this into a sort of jingle:

> The aroused
> looks to the arouser
> for the sign of arousal
> promising intimacy
> the only peace of desire.

Perhaps the whole philosophical tradition took a wrong turn at the point where we asked, 'What is "just wanting"?' Philosophers paid more attention to the fact that when I want something *I am without it* than to the much more important fact that wanting stems from feeling good. (You're not hungry when you're not well. And discovering a purpose in life has been known to improve the appetite.) Thus they concluded that 'just wanting' was 'just being without', that is, being empty.

And when you think this way, what is there so special in wanting another person? If wanting is not the awakening of my good feeling of myself, there are no grounds for specially wanting another person who will *exercise* this good feeling by wanting me.

It may be because of this early mistake that the philosophical tradition has had so little to say about interpersonal relations, about intimacy, intersubjectivity – a pretty hefty omission!

The importance of Freud was that he discovered the positive nature of the 'just wanting' state. In place of the presumed hole or *tabula rasa* that was thought to precede our definite, articulate desires, Freud found a huge sea of delight, the oceanic dream of self, which people are living out, sometimes tragically and disastrously, sometimes hopefully, sometimes creatively and holily.

The scholastic philosophical tradition has something to say about the 'just wanting' state. It says that the will is attracted to 'the good in general' in the first place, and that what is happening when you want something is that this general orientation to the good is being narrowed down to the particular. But what could 'the good in general' *as an object* be? Austin Farrer, a brilliant, difficult, and waggish English philosopher, says of the scholastic theory, 'Anyone can see that this is a lie.' That's in *Finite and Infinite* (which is being reprinted after about thirty years – maybe a sign of the book's importance).

Because of the emphasis placed on the desiring person's *not having* what he/she desires, Socrates was able to tie his young friend Agathon up in knots, in Plato's great dialogue on love, *The Symposium*. Each of the guests at the dinner party has made a speech in praise of love, and Agathon has been the most fulsome in its praises, saying that love is the most beautiful thing in the world. Socrates asks him whether someone who loves (or desires – same word in Greek, *eros*) something has it or not. Agathon replies not. Socrates asks whether the lover desires what is beautiful or what is not. Agathon replies, 'What is beautiful'. 'So love desires beauty?' asks Socrates, beginning to close his argument. 'Surely,' says the innocent Agathon. The dialogue proceeds:

'But didn't we agree that the lover desires what he doesn't have?'
'Yes.'
'So love doesn't have beauty.'
'I suppose not.'
'So how can you say that something that doesn't have beauty is the most beautiful thing in the world?'
'Socrates, I didn't know what I was talking about.'
'Still, it was a beautiful speech, Agathon!'

3.

A moment of honesty

I call for a moment of reflective honesty in myself and in my reader. Have I not, all my life and before all else, desired to be desired?

I want simply to give full acknowledgement to the fact that yes, I have wanted all along to be desired, found attractive. Not to evaluate that fact, simply to recognize it.

Something begins to be very clear when I do face this fact. The desire to be desired stems from the certainty of being desirable: for it is *wanting to experience my desirability in action*, wanting the *exercise* of my most satisfying 'habit' (habitus), proclivity, propensity or whatever. Once allow doubt as to the *existence* of this propensity or potential, and the desire I am speaking of evaporates. You might as well, then, speak of a desire for orgasm on the part of an asexual being.

This exercising, by a lover's touch, of my desirability, is the meaning of a caress.

Now there is a reason why I have this implicit certainty of being desirable. This certainty flows directly and necessarily out of self-awareness. Since to be is to be good, consciously to be is to be, consciously, desirable.

Since, then, being desired exercises my desirability, and since my desirability is my being, that which exercises my desirability is exercising my being.

Now all my desire heads toward a *total* exercise of my being, of my sense of myself as desirable. To be fully actual is what all, unknowingly, seek.

What could my total actualization, or exercise, or stretching be? Well, if it were possible to *experience my creation*, that would surely be an experience of total actualization. But here a difficulty arises. That which exercises my desirability-propensity is *being desired* by someone – this and this alone. How would *experiencing my creation* be *experiencing myself as desired*? The answer is that the desire for me that I would then be aware of is that desire which makes its object, that love creative of its object, which is God. The desire for me, which alone awakens my desirability, is the desire for me to be, which is why I am.

Thus not only do we all desire to be desired. At the deepest level, we all desire to be desired to be.

And we must surely wonder why the experience of orgasm is called 'coming'. Is it that its intensity, compared with the drabness of ordinary awareness, suggests coming into being as the essence of ecstasy? It would be interesting to find the equivalents for this shadow word in other languages. Has metaphysics found its way into the language written mainly on walls?

4.

What is self-awareness?

The expression 'self-awareness' suggests having myself as the *object* of my awareness. It really means the opposite of this: myself as the *subject* of awareness. Self-awareness is something I bring, and have to bring, to every act of thought or feeling or decision. It is my end, the me-end, of everything I do. Wherever there is awareness, there is self-awareness. Awareness *is* self-awareness. The self, aware, is self-aware. Thus a person is self-aware all the time except for periods of deep dreamless sleep.

Whatever you are aware of, *you* are aware. This is self-awareness.

All religion, all spirituality, is based on and addressed to this primal knowledge that is the heart of all our experience. It is, however, not easy – at least at first – to come into touch with our 'first knowing'. Normally it is *either* buried *or* is moving into 'second knowing'. Meditation techniques attempt to get us into a *third* way, of *being* in our first knowing. Second knowing is always of something definite. First knowing is a simple knowing*ness* of nothing in particular. That is why it is our contact-point with the infinite, the nothing-in-particular that is God.

Ordinary consciousness is a confused mixture of self-awareness and reflective self-awareness, of thinking *with* myself and thinking *of* myself. And the thinking *of* myself is multicoloured by societal expectations, roles, etc. In the dream, the confusion is tidied up. For there, self-awareness is the dreamer, the characters of the dream are aspects of the self as reflected upon and commented on by society, of the self as presented to others. This is a neat arrangement. The only snag is that we don't easily understand what is thus arranged!

There follow twelve examples showing the process from first knowing to second:

1. What happens when you understand something you didn't understand before? Isn't it really a passage from 'knowing' to

10

'knowing you know'? That is why, when you are trying to get someone to understand something, you say, cajolingly, 'You know, you do know.' You can *see* he or she knows, only he can't.

2. Plato with the slave and the triangle. Plato (in the role of Socrates) had a *hunch* that we know already and all that education does is bring this out. But, not having reached our degree of introspection, the only way for him to *say* that we know it already was to say that we know the *object* already, as a kind of ideal triangle or whatever in the soul, waiting to be matched up with the triangle we see. He wasn't on to the kind of knowing that is self-awareness. Aquinas got further than Plato. Instead of having in ourselves ideal triangles, etc., we are, as it were, *light* which, until it falls on an object, does not become understanding. But when the light falls on some image the teacher puts before us, we say, 'Aha!' We have passed from knowing to knowing we know. For Archimedes the 'light' fell on the rising level of his bathwater, and he ran naked through the streets shouting, 'I got it!'

3. Aristotle says that when people watch a drama they learn nothing new. They are put freshly in touch with what they already know.

4. Self-deception. Herbert Fingarette wrote a book by this name. In it he sought to avoid the *apparent* meaning of 'self-deception' which is that I have two selves, one deceiving the other – which is nonsense. (In a similar way, 'self-awareness' *seems* to mean 'my self' (no. 1) looking at 'my self' (no. 2) – which is nonsense.) What self-deception really is, he concluded, is inhibiting the process whereby I move from 'knowing' to 'knowing I know'. What causes self-deception is generally fear in one form or another. A striking and notorious example is the German people saying they 'did not know' about the concentration camps. They knew, in the sense of a miserable self-awareness, a feeling of something terribly wrong. Out of fear, they did not let this knowing pass to 'knowing knowing'. Far worse, of course, was the self-inhibition practised by the criminals themselves. It is said that Albert Von Speer never admitted it to himself.

The current peace movement is an excellent example. We have 'known' about nuclear weapons for thirty years. Only recently something has happened to make people know they know. When you just 'know', you are passive. When you know you know, you feel you have to do something, get out there.

5. When a friend tells you that you are being difficult in some

11

way, it does not come as a complete surprise. If it did, you wouldn't know what you had to correct.

6. When I look back on something incredibly foolish that I did in the past, I may feel that I didn't know what I was doing. But of course I did; I wasn't acting in my sleep! But I didn't know as I know now. I knew what I was doing, but I didn't know I knew.

7. 'I told her she was in love with me, and it blew her away.' So real is our 'first knowing' or self-awareness, that it is sometimes apparent to another before the person brings it to 'second knowing'.

8. The strange thing called premonition is another good example. Sometimes one senses an impending event in one's first knowing before it explodes into everyone's second knowing.

9. Trying to remember something. Augustine asks, 'How do we know we've *nearly* got it when we haven't yet got it. What have we nearly got?' Compared by George Eliot to trying to sneeze. The strange orgasm of mind.

10. The déjà-vu experience. 'I have been here before.' First knowing is changing all the time. Sometimes an experience, especially a smell, evokes an earlier first knowing which, getting attached to the present experience, produces the feeling that we have had *this* experience before.

11. When I nearly lose someone, I realize how much that person means to me. First knowing, or first feeling, is forced by events into the area of second knowing.

12. An important insight of modern therapy is that a person can come to the point of being able to say, 'I *chose* to become the person I am'.

5.

Self-awareness is self-affirming

Having grasped the true nature of self-awareness, we see that self-awareness is self-affirming. If self-awareness means *looking* at myself, this does not follow. I may not like what I see, but I cannot possibly dislike who I am. For self-awareness means being *with* myself, and I cannot be *with* myself indifferently. 'With' means with. With myself, I am for myself.

To get a right idea about human beings, think about a bird. Then think of its simply being itself, its 'birding', as conscious. To get a screwed-up idea of what consciousness does to the human animal, think of a bird suddenly mutating, collapsing, unbirding. Bernard Lonergan says that in the conscious being, consciousness adds nothing to being. Conscious beings *are* consciously. And this means that all the energy that goes into making a being be itself is, in the human being, conscious energy. This conscious energy is the belief that every person has in him/herself.

Self-awareness is self-believing. Being myself is believing in myself. I cannot be without believing in myself. In so far as I *am* myself I *believe* in myself. I can no more stop believing in myself than a bird can unbird or the sea cease to be sea. Conscious being believes in itself in the act of being conscious. 'I am myself' means 'I do myself, I promote myself, I "self" myself,' as Gerard Manley Hopkins ceaselessly stressed.

Self-awareness is self-affirming. This is of the utmost importance for the understanding of ourselves and for the building of our theology.

We easily miss this. For most of our problems come from *not* believing in ourselves, having a poor idea of ourselves. Most therapy is addressed to our poor self-image, even our self-hatred.

But if you reflect on your own problem of self-disesteem – and we all have one – I think you will find that self-disesteem consists in not allowing your fundamental sense of yourself to come through

13

and prevail. And therapy is addressed, precisely, *to* this fundamental good sense of self, seeking to coax it out. In other words, therapy is built on the supposition that a good sense of self *is already there* in everyone: that it is who the person really is: that the worse the person appears in her or his own eyes, the more this goodness is buried – but it is the essential self nonetheless.

In fact, just as no correction of my behaviour by another is possible unless I already know what the person is talking about, so no emotional healing of me is possible unless I already have a good sense of myself for it to build on.

Though we are not too much in touch with it, our sense of ourselves as good and desirable is *far more fundamental* in us than anything else we may think about ourselves. And though we aren't much in touch with this sense, we very much take it for granted. I mean, *ask* yourself, 'Am I a desirable person?' and you will probably feel sheepish, especially if you're talking with someone else. But have someone you love turn you down, and the rage and pain you feel shows that you *do* think of yourself as desirable and *therefore* are hurt at not being desired.

Now it is *on* the belief in myself that is built into self-awareness that all my relationships are based. It is only because I feel desirable that I like someone else in the first place. And it is only because I feel desirable that I want that person to desire me.

These two statements need explaining. First of all, when you feel drawn to another person, that is your own sense of your goodness expanding. There is always, in the attraction to another, the feeling of a larger life opening up in myself. I *am* more in being drawn to another. And the reason why I then want that other to feel drawn to me is that my awakening sense of *being* desirable wants to be completed by my *being* desired.

This sense of myself as desirable is the basis of all my relating. For it is the heart of desiring. It is because I am desirable that I am desire-able.

This sense of myself as desirable is also that in me which seeks God. My sense of myself as endless reaches out, or in, toward an infinite *idea* of myself.

The first of the above two facts is expounded in the First Quadrant; the second fact, in the Second Quadrant.

14

6.

To be is to feel good

Now if self-awareness precedes and undergirds all *thinking* about myself, if I *consciously am* before I am able to say that I am this or that, then also I *consciously want* before I am able to say that I want this or that. As all my thinking about myself and my life depends upon a prior presence of myself to myself, so all my desiring depends on a prior *affective* presence of myself to myself.

Before I find myself saying to myself, 'I am this person and I want this or that,' I consciously and desirously am.

As my basic *awareness* of myself grounds all that I come to *know*, so my basic *love* of myself grounds all that I come to *want*.

All our desiring is the attempt of an original feeling-good, an original hedonic sense of myself, to extend itself, to realize itself over the wider field of interaction with others. All desiring is the attempt to realize the dream of myself, of a self-in-bliss which was my original condition in the physical, then the psychic, womb. All desiring is the attempt to be happy, the attempt of an original happiness to extend into the particulars of life.

My original desire is for I know not what. It is undifferentiated. It is for I know not what *because* it is an original happy state of myself not yet knowing how to extend itself. The state of not knowing what I want is not to be compared to an emptiness, a hole waiting to be filled. It is a state of happiness not knowing where to go to extend itself.

Thus we uncover a principle that is the basis of the whole of our self-understanding and of our relating to others and to what we call God. *We desire not because we are empty but because we are full.* (In so far as we 'con' ourselves – and we easily do – into feeling empty, desire is replaced by demand, the compulsive sucking-into-itself of a vacuum. We shall meet this in the third quadrant. It need not detain us here.)

Desiring is the extension of a basic sense of being desirable. This

15

is much clearer and more vivid to us when our desire goes out to another person, not to money or the latest in rapid-moving hardware. When you feel attracted to a person, you feel good. You are aroused from psychological sleep to a fuller life of yourself.

The breakthrough of Freud, giving birth to the psychoanalytic age, was the discovery of the vast world of desire before desire for this or that, the discovery of our desiring in its original molten state before it cools into the distinct objectives. Freud discovered what I have called, above, the dream of myself – which, not surprisingly, shows itself in my dreams. Unfortunately, Freud called what he had discovered 'the unconscious'. Because he made the common mistake of thinking of self-awareness as having oneself as object of awareness, he had to call the fundamental condition that precedes all our activity '*un*conscious'.

16

7.

The self, feeling, is the self felt

It is often said, 'You are what you do.' It is much truer to say, 'You are what you feel.' It is in feeling happy, or angry, or sad, or hopeful, in response to an event, that I touch base with myself. My *identity* lights up in one of these *feelings*. Who I am can become known to others, and to myself, far more accurately by how I feel than by the image I may form of myself. 'He's angry as hell about something – wish I could find out what it is!' is the way a person will often find themself posing the question, 'Who *is* this person whom I'm getting to know?'

An important contemporary psychoanalyst in the Freudian school, Alexander Lowen, argues in a recent book that the narcissistic personality is one who has been in the habit, since earliest and pre-remembered childhood, of thinking of him/herself *not* as 'feeling this' or 'feeling that' but as 'the person I think of myself as'. I have taken on, 'internalized' my mother's image of me, have made this image my own, *to the displacement* of my own spontaneous, firsthand, feeling-response to what happens around me. As my mother's image was one of adoration, my self-image is essentially grandiose.

It follows from this that what I shall expect from others is not *response to the feeling I show*, but recognition of the grandiose person I conceive myself to be. And since I am not identifying myself by my feelings, I am not going to have any sense of the feelings of others.

The narcissist, then, is one who is out of touch with his/her true self, with the self that shows itself from moment to moment in feeling. He is fixated on a self of his own imaging.

Am I talking about you? Certainly I am talking about me. Narcissism seems to be joining the passive-aggressive syndrome as the common cold of modern psychology.

The point is that this narcissism can be identified and to some extent prevented from displacing something which we do experience

17

as much more basically who we are: the self of feeling, the self that can get mad as hell and that can sit excitedly by the telephone, the self that wants things.

Now if I am identified with my image of myself, my sense of who I am is essentially private – I'm looking at myself, I've got myself hung in my picture gallery. But if I am identified with the strong feeling that I am at this moment displaying to you, then my sense of myself is not private but exposed to you. And if this strong feeling is a good feeling toward you, then it is a good feeling. And a good feeling is feeling good. Thus what feels good in myself in liking you is what I am offering you to like. Thus the self-liking self is the heart of the feelings that occur between persons, so that all those feelings are the phases or modes or complexifications of the self-liking self's desire to be enjoyed by others. For the narcissist in us, on the other hand, the imaged self is always aloof from the scene, fearful of not receiving its due measure of adoration.

As the self, aware, is self-aware, so the self, feeling is the self felt. We feel ourselves in feeling what happens to us. 'How does it feel, not knowing whether you've got the job?' means 'How do *you* feel, not knowing etc.?' What's the mood *of you* that you are now going through?

You are what you are feeling at this moment. This understanding of the self has recently been put to use in a brilliant new therapeutic technique known as 'focusing', described by Eugene T. Gendlin in a book with that title. What he means by focusing is this. Something happens, something disturbing or perhaps hopeful, and I ask myself, 'How do I feel?' Almost certainly a mixture of feelings, even conflicting feelings. Well, which is the most important of these feelings? Can I say what the whole problem I've run into feels like? I choose one – say 'disappointment'. I *focus* on that one. I bring my mass of feeling to that focus. Then I try to 'listen' to that feeling – as though it were my true self wanting to speak; which it is. If the right word or image comes, I experience a 'body shift', a release of tension.

Now this whole process consists in allowing my body to tell me how I am. It is a repetition of what self-awareness originally is: animal consciousness breaking into words. And it is the opposite, the turning-back, of another whole way of self-envisaging that is narcissistic: a self-image imposing itself on me imperviously to my own immediate, primitive self-feeling.

An important new theory about the origin of narcissism, or of the narcissist tendency in all of us, is as follows. Somewhere around the second year, when we have begun to acquire an elementary sense of separateness from the mother through the exercise of motor skills and the beginning-control of bowel and urinary functions, the child feels a strong need to 'return to base', to mother, and a new affective bond begins to grow. Then the mother needs to be very comfortable with a certain ambiguity: a combination, all in one act, of supporting the child and pushing the child away. To the extent that the mother fails here, the child gets the message, 'Love me or leave me'. He faces the unbearable alternatives of becoming part of mother again and being out in the cold. Thus he won't develop that good sense of self which comes with a strongly supported independence. So he will depend, for the sense of who he is, *not* on an immediate inner vitality but on an image of himself, primarily of course the mother's.

Unfortunately, the narcissistic personality thus formed in the earliest years is heavily endorsed by our society with its heavy emphasis on *imaging ourselves*. The vast, technologically empowered world of advertizing stresses day and night the importance of being with the 'right' people, in the 'right' clothes, in the 'right' car, in the 'right' job, etc. I must be forever improving my image, learning more and more to see myself *in* the image of the good life.

Once we begin to understand what it is *in us* that lets all this phony stuff in, we begin to see that we can overcome it. These voices of the culture, powerful though they are, are addressing a person who does not exist, namely a person who is known in the first place through a self-formed image, a person who is 'hung' in his/her own gallery. They are addressed to my non-existence, to my non-person. They thrive in the void of self-feeling.

In short, narcissism is not 'having a grand image of myself as opposed to a modest image'. It is 'seeing myself in an image as opposed to feeling myself'.

8.

The structure of intimacy

The sense of myself as good is foundational. We now have to see it at work in the forming of the bond between persons. Let us look at the initial forming of an intimate relationship between John and Mary, discerning its dynamic.

John desires Mary, is attracted toward her. That's all the datum so far. John, desiring Mary, is under her power – for goodness, beauty in a person, *is* power.

But also, John, desiring Mary, is awakening to his sense of his own goodness, to *his* power.

Thus in coming under *her* power, *he* feels powerful: his newfound sense of power is being called into play *in* his attraction to Mary.

It follows that if his desire for her is to be fulfilled, this will be through the *exercise* of his newfound sense of power.

But this can happen only if Mary, attracted toward him, comes under *his* power.

Thus precisely in coming under Mary's power through desiring her, John's own power increases. His desire for her is desire for his own power to be exercised over her. In other words, the power we want to exercise over each other is the power we *awaken* in each other.

That is the basic structure. Here are some remarks. Today we are very preoccupied with power. We hear of politicians' power as gaining and waning almost daily. We hear of manipulation and 'bondage' and God knows what else besides. What desperately needs to be understood is that people's *essential* power over each other, which is the power of their beauty and goodness, cannot be thought of as the possession of each, but has to be thought of as a life-force whose interest it is to unite them. My power is my partnership in the energy that unites persons in love. The essential human power is not solitary but unifying.

But when we speak of an energy or a life-force, we easily create

20

the impression of a force that welds people together with them passive to it. The exact opposite is the case. The force is *in* each, *as* the beauty/power of each. And because it *awakes* in each the attraction toward the other, it is, in each, the movement toward communion.

That which, in each person, urges toward communion is the basic fact about desire, namely that it stems from feeling good.

On this fact the whole understanding of the human reality rests.

What we are looking at now, in fact, is the universal interhuman significance of that 'first OK sense of separate existence' which we acquire with the mother's 'gentle push'. It is that essential good feeling of ourselves that is foundational to our life as friends, as lovers, as parents, as ministers, etc.

> The beauty of a person
> is another's to unfold
> and is the other's unfolding:
> the cause of desire
> admitting to desiring
> admits the desiring
> to intimacy.
> No man, says Donne, is an island
> entire of itself: the entirety of one
> is in another's holding
> intended to be relaxed
> as the beauty of the first
> overpowers: everywhere
> beauty is in relation
> and persons' essence
> is in constant exchange.

Risking banality to make the point, here it is in the form of a Victorian music-hall refrain:

> Desiring you / awakens me
> To what you may see / in me.

The diagram illustrates the process of two people (John and Mary) becoming intimate. Each person is represented by two concentric circles. The outer band is outgoing desire, the being attracted toward another person. The arrows, accordingly, move outward. The 'inside' of this attraction is the person's sense of him/herself as good. It is represented by the inner circle. The arrows on the inner

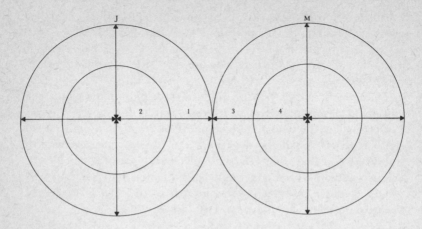

circle go inward, for my conscious goodness wants to draw the other toward me.

Let us say, then, that the first thing to happen is that John feels drawn to Mary. Mark the appropriate arrow 1. With that, John's own sense of his goodness is intensified. Mark the appropriate arrow 2.

It is here that things become interesting, and seemingly paradoxical. For since John's subjection to Mary's power or charm intensifies his sense of his own, the completion of his subjection to hers will be in her succumbing to his. Let us say that this happens. Mark the appropriate arrow 3. This awakening of Mary to John will in its turn involve her awakening to herself, which gives us the fourth arrow, marked 4.

As the relationship develops, it becomes clearer and clearer that the subjection of John to Mary is but the obverse of the subjection of Mary to John. They are the two sides of a single surrender to a life-process.

Further, they are surrendering to the process not as animals surrender to the process that advances itself through their mating and procreating, but as conscious participants in a mystery that is drawing them *through* their feeling of self and other, through the law of the person whereby to be drawn to another is to draw the other to oneself, the law represented by the two concentric circles.

9.

Intimacy not a romantic concept

The idea of intimacy that we are elaborating is not romantic. That is to say, we are not regarding the intimacy between two persons as something that just happens for no known reason – 'Marriages are made in heaven'. On the contrary, there is a solid basis for intimacy in the very constitution of the human person as a being in desire, as aroused and arousing. When these two basic factors of desire come 'into phase', are 'in synch', we have the beginning of intimacy.

And when we analyse the process whereby they come into phase, we begin to sense the essential mystery of the person, which lies in the fact that a person is unique and of absolute value in him/herself yet has his/her flourishing or full existence in the power of another, which power needs to be balanced by the power of the first. What we really discover is, that when we try to give a full description of a person's existence we find ourselves talking about two persons! To talk about a subject or person is to talk about intersubjectivity. Desire, which is the shaping and driving force of the person, is fulfilled only in intimacy.

Thus human beings, beings in desire, in-exist one another, or they remain less than human, unfulfilled in essence. This is the universal fact about human beings. This it is which comes into play when two persons become intimate. When persons become intimate, they become what persons are. They actualize that mutual in-existence which is the essence of personhood. When two people become intimate, they join the human race.

This makes it quite impossible to regard the two intimates as making a private corner for themselves, carving out an existence of their own in the midst of a heartless world. This is why I say that intimacy cannot be regarded as a romantic notion. Intimacy should be regarded not as an insulation against a heartless world, but on the contrary as a wholesome contagion in a heartless world. This is brought about by the fact that, since the beginning of human time, the primordial intimacy, which is of man and woman, has been public and acclaimed and creates what we call a home, not only for the children but also for neighbours and, in some radiant instances (and, be it noted, in some cultures though not ours) for anyone in need of food and human comfort.

But the most important implication of this viewpoint is that we cannot stop regarding mutual in-existence as something that, miraculously and unaccountably, sometimes 'just happens' (the romantic view). Rather we have to see it as something more like a skill, a virtue (= a power), that can and should be developed. A person can become more attentive to self and to other in more and more encounters. One can create the optimal conditions for some degree of intimacy (and of course there *are* degrees – many of them) to occur. This is the charism of Leo Buscaglia.

And far from the style of Leo Buscaglia being a secular substitute for the *religious* bond between people, it is the actualizing of the *natural* bond between people which is what makes people begin to feel God in their midst. Precisely the reason why so much gospelling of people – stopping the busy stranger in the shopping mall and asking, 'Have you accepted Jesus Christ as your personal saviour?' – is counterproductive, is that it neglects, overlooks, bypasses, short-circuits the natural bond between people which is God's primary witness to him/herself in the world. To call Jesus Christ into an absence of inter-human feeling is to reverse his own direction into the world of men and women.

And because we have to regard intimacy not as something that 'just happens' but as the intense realization of the universal essence of human being, we have to say that it is not just intimacy that leads to God but the universal human mystery of which intimacy is the intense actualization. We are mysterious mutually in-existent beings, whose life makes much fuller sense as the response to a divine 'pull'. A very ancient anthropology (made use of by St Paul) describes the human being as composed of three, not two, elements: body, soul, and spirit. We might paraphrase this: substance, life, and inter-life. People got into a tangle here by suggesting that the 'spirit' here is the Holy Spirit, God, in other words. In fact there is a very ancient formula which says that the human is composed of 'body, soul, and Holy Spirit'. And it isn't always easy to see when Paul means, by 'spirit', 'the Holy Spirit', and when he means the human spirit.

What is really important and exciting here is what *gives rise* to the confusion, namely: Spirit, inter-life, the mysterious energy that flows between persons, is what opens us to God. It is at once the opening of our *desire* to God and God's *point of entry* into us; our way of opening, God's way of entering.

There is a tendency today, on the part of the growing number of people who are breaking out of the straitjacket of 'scientism' and discovering the all-pervading energy, to identify this energy with God. This is very natural but, I think, a mistake and a fore-shortening of the mystery that these people are beginning to discover. I would say that this energy is our *human* greatness, that human greatness which is what stretches beyond itself to God. The more you are, the more you desire. The greater we are the more we desire. Or, as the gospel puts it, 'to him that hath shall be given'. A great deal of debate today about whether there is a God is pretty hopeless because *both* parties – the believer as well as the non-believer – are assuming that the need for God springs from a sense of worthlessness on our part, the implication being that a sense of human greatness would make God redundant. The exact opposite is the case. A sense of human worthlessness makes God unbelievable; a sense of human greatness is the threshold of belief.

The threshold of belief is that special sense of human greatness which is had in the experience of our larger, intersubjective life. And we only really sense this larger intersubjective life when we understand the intimacy between two persons as a glimpse or fore-taste of a universal human unity.

25

10.

On the philosophic map (1)

The perennial philosophy was concerned, above all, to understand desire as involving not only the desiring individual and the desired object, but the total reality within which the experience of desire happens. When I desire anything, there is taking place in me that movement toward the good or desirable which is the dynamic of all being – of all human being certainly, and by a very acceptable metaphoric extension, of all being.

How the philosophers in this tradition explain this universal connectedness of my desire with the total rhythm of the cosmos was not nearly as satisfying as was the intuition that this connection exists. As we have seen, the standard story is that the will, or radical appetite of conscious beings, is desirous of 'the good in general', of the good as good, of sheer goodness, and that it is this *general* inclination that empowers my inclination toward the *particular* good object that is presented to me.

To understand the vital connection, to understand all desiring as the desiring of all goodness, another route, I believe, has to be taken.

First of all, the source of all our desiring is the sense *of ourselves* as good, as desirable. My desire for an object is this sense of myself presented with an opportunity to continue and to expand. This is much clearer when the object is another person. The use of the term 'arousal' to describe erotic excitement expresses the profound insight into myself, that in feeling attracted strongly to another I awaken from relative sleep into a new fullness of well-being.

But this awakened sense of my goodness has not yet, at this stage, revealed its real significance for the understanding of desire. This is crucially important, so let me labour the point.

At the 'arousal' stage, my sense of my goodness has awakened, delightfully, in a movement of desire *that puts me in the other person's power*. That is entirely proper at this stage. But if I stay there, I come into a relationship of dependence that will be good for neither of us.

What needs to happen next, if the relationship is to develop, is that the other be attracted by *my* charm, my allure, my goodness, and thus *come under my power*. This mutual empowerment is the condition of *interdependence*, which has to displace dependence if a relationship is to grow. In an interdependent relationship, each is affirming, is accepting, is appropriating, his or her own goodness as *working* in the relationship.

This new moment, of self-acceptance in a love relationship, is the crucial moment. It is the watershed in all human relations. It is what most of us most of the time stop short of. For this is the vital point at which our belief in our goodness is not strong enough to carry us forward. It is always some, often subtle, self-rejection that hinders us from believing in another's finding us attractive and from seeing that the other does so when this happens.

Our sense of our goodness, that easily awakes to the beauty of another, fails when it comes to supporting the other's awakening to ourselves.

And thus our weak sense of our goodness holds us short of interdependent relationships, and keeps us in dependent relationships. We are willing slaves to beauty rather than sharers in beauty.

Now most important for our present concern is this. At the first, or arousal stage, my sense of my goodness has not yet revealed its essential role in the dynamic of desire. Filling the scene is the allure of the other, to which I am being drawn like a piece of metal to a magnet – I mean, I easily think of it that way because *my* role has not yet appeared. If you ask me what I am drawn by, I reply, 'His/her charm'. I do not bother to add, or even notice, that his/her charm draws me *by* my sense of my goodness. To use a crude analogy just to get the language straight: I see a bull being led around, and you ask me: 'What's it being led by?' and I reply, 'By the man pulling it along of course.' I don't think of saying, 'It is being led by the nose.' And certainly, if you ask me this question about my own infatuation, I answer with a list of the beloved's charms: I do not answer, 'By the nose.'

Now at the first, dependency stage, desire is much easier to talk about. The as yet unobtrusive presence of my own sense of being good leaves the other's charm the only force in the field. And so the simple magnet-model for desire easily inserts itself.

This, I suggest, is how the simple magnet-model comes to impose

27

itself, unnoticed, on philosophy. The philosopher's image of desire is 'someone being drawn to someone or something by the latter's allure'. Entirely in the shade is 'someone being drawn to someone or something, out of his/her own sense of being good'.

Now we must go on to describe the relationship when it is becoming increasingly one of interdependence. My attraction toward the other person is now much stronger, empowered by the other's manifestation and avowal of attraction to me. I have a sort of jingle for naming this process:

> The aroused
> looks to the arouser
> for the sign of arousal
> which admits to intimacy,
> the only peace of desire.

But whilst my desire for the other is now stronger, it is also more complex. What I want is no longer simply 'the other person as a constant and predictable source of attraction'. What I want is the progress of a relationship through the growing mutual exposure of the other and myself. In a very real sense, *my* desire has another subject besides the subject that is myself. And it has another object besides the other person, namely the unpredictable interaction whereby the relationship deepens. Thus, in place of the predictable (or at least treated as predictable) object, my desire now embraces the object in a wider context of a shared unpredictable interaction.

What this means is that my desire has now become an investment of myself in a developing shared life, a commitment of myself to the unpredictable in hope. In fact my desire has developed into hope. The goodness that I sense as mine is now being invested in an ongoing, risk-laden, unpredictable, enormously promising interplay of *two* goodnesses.

Now whether I recognize this clearly or not, this new, deeper and more exacting direction of my desire is bringing me into a *new* dependence: a dependence on whatever it is that sustains hope. Above all, it is a dependence on the total mystery that constitutes me, this unique good person, and supports my investment of my goodness in the risk-laden adventure of intimacy. The anchor of my new hope is goodness itself. This bears out a principle that I have come to see as bedrock to our whole quest for God: namely that we look to God, in hope, to the extent that we are investing ourselves in life's value and beauty, and not out of a *poor* sense of ourselves or a disappointed sense for life.

Now it is this dependence of desire-become-hope on the total mystery of our being, on goodness itself, that is *the way* in which our desire, aroused by the particular good that is another person, is connected with goodness as a whole, with goodness as total embracing and supporting mystery. The connection with universal goodness is through the growth of desire into hope that comes with a breakthrough of desire into intersubjectivity. Hope is desire in the skilled hands of God. We begin to feel those 'skilled hands', probably unknowingly, as the encompassing mystery on which lovers, and all adventurers, lean.

It is as hope that desire is impelled toward goodness itself, toward the absolute good that is the original cause of desire. It is hopelessly unsatisfactory to see this radical impulsion as the desire for *absolute* goodness being fobbed-off, as it were, with *particular* goods. Yet it is this latter model that has dominated Christian asceticism.

The reason it has done so is, as I have already suggested, because it is based on an idea of desire that is so much simpler − and the mind is lazy, especially where the spiritual is concerned, and goes for the easy formula. Desire is likened to the metal pulled by the magnet: so there is the pull of the particular object, and there is the pull of 'the good', and somehow we have to fit them together. But the real pull undergoes subtle and profound transformations; from the simple pull of the beautiful other, through the phases and hazards of a relationship, to the pull of the mystery itself, the subtle 'come on' of a power utterly beyond our mind's grasp but able to communicate with us through love.

Thus there is a *progression* from the simple pull of the particular to the pull of the good in itself, and this progression does not consist in the *leaving-behind* of the particular, but, on the contrary, in the coming with the particular into desire's fuller existence which is hope, wherein may be sensed the touch of the good in itself. For all its haunting beauty, Diotima's famous teaching of Socrates at the end of *The Symposium* conveys the former idea. Particular beauties are all left behind to arrive at Beauty itself.

There is a thinker/teacher of our time who especially merits attention in the context of a deepened and extended notion of desire, Leo Buscaglia. For the genius of Buscaglia is to have fastened on the crucial moment that I am highlighting, the moment a relationship tends to stop short of, and the moment we all stop short of in our dealings with each other; namely the moment when I believe in myself enough to invite the other's being-attracted to me or rejecting me. This is the moment when we step beyond dependence into interdependence, and feel the human mystery. It is the moment when desire becomes hope and connects me with the mystery. It is the moment when the Body that is Christ can become reality. It is the moment by staying safely short of which the world is dying. Buscaglia seems to me to exemplify, in a way that is wholly pragmatic and free of the debasement of spirituality by religion, the primary truth about desire as our opening to the Spirit that makes us one. He has discovered the spiritual grammar in Jesus' statement that the peacemakers are the children of God.

Another ally is Austin Farrer. In *Finite and Infinite* there is a section titled: 'Will the clue to the nature of desire'. The meaning of this phrase is that desire reveals its true nature when it comes into the moment of decision, either for the new initiative of self-exposure that makes possible interdependence or for the cowardice that overshadows our society. Love is desire decided for.

But the simplistic image of desire persists, of a pull by the object as opposed to the arousal of the subject. 'Porrige nucem puero!' says Augustine. Put nuts before a small boy and he'll grab one. 'Trahit sua quemque voluptas.' Yes – provided one reflects deeply on the nature of voluptas, of arousal, of the awakening self. But it is so much simpler to concentrate on the nut.

In fact, we could sum it up by applying to desire what Lonergan has said, unforgettably, about knowing. The empiricist, he says, thinks that what is most obvious about knowing is what knowing obviously is. And it's not. It's infinitely elusive and wonderful. So is desire.

Let me now try to get all this into a more succinct form. Desire is most nearly itself when, asserting my own goodness which is its source, I pass from dependence to interdependence whose soul is hope. Then is desire most itself, so then am I most drawn – no longer by the obvious charm of another, but by the mystery that brings us together enlarging desire into hope.

The mistake in Diotima's progression to absolute beauty lies in misinterpreting the unimportance of the beautiful body in the moment of transcendence. The beauty that draws me into dependence (the first phase) becomes less important in ceasing to be the one important thing through the coming-on-the-scene of *two* poles, the other's charm over me and my charm over the other. The single infatuating body is not *left behind* on the journey onward, but becomes the partner to a relationship whose whole health is in going onward.

And in pointing to this weakness in Diotima's account of the progression, we are pointing to the great weakness in the whole philosophical tradition, 'perennial' and otherwise; the assumption, so widespread and old that it is difficult to point to, that the experience to be penetrated and elaborated on is that of the single subject, never of subjects in communion, each in the other, each having his/her life in the other's power.

This lacuna is most strangling when it comes to theology. For it is the ability of persons to be in each other, and the fact that short of being in each other they are barely persons, that is how we are the manifestation of a Godhead that is persons in one another in one essence.

If I may be permitted another jingle:

> When desire must grope
> there arises hope
> whose subtle pull
> is on life at the full
> opening its doors
> to desire's first cause.

The Second Quadrant

11.

Introducing the second quadrant

Normally a person feels their desirability *indirectly*, in the process of desiring another or of being drawn by a prospect or project. The person's desirableness is felt, as it were, 'off' the encounter with the other. Desirability is the source of desiring, but it is the product (desiring) that is directly perceived, the source indirectly, rather as we know a sickness by the symptoms it is producing.

Now there is an experience of feeling one's desirability, one's core-selfhood, *directly*, not through the medium of desiring another or being drawn by some exciting project or prospect.

When this happens, desire is certainly felt, because the *source* of desire (the person's sense of being desirable) is being activated.

But this desire has no object. It arises precisely not in the context of being drawn to someone or something in particular.

Now all desire is desire for intimacy, for a fulfilling situation of being with another or being part of some great project. Desire is for fuller life.

Therefore *this* desire for nothing in particular, coming out of a direct sensing of one's desirability, is a desire for intimacy.

With whom, or with what, could this intimacy be? With whatever it is that is awakening the person's self-awareness as desirable. And what could that be? The awakening comes not from outside – there is no object – but from inside. It is an awakening of the self at its very core, in its very essence as desirable. What then could be its source?

Well, to speak of the essence of my desirableness is to speak of the 'why' of it, of why I am desirable, of what makes me desirable. So it is with 'what makes me desirable' that I seek intimacy.

Now a reality with which *intimacy* is desired must be capable of intimacy. And only a *desirous* being is capable of intimacy. Therefore we must in some sense attribute to this mysterious reality desire.

So what we get is 'a desiring reality that makes me desirable'.

35

And what could that be which makes desirable what it desires, but the reality we call God?

God is the inverse of reality as we know it. We know a thing because it exists. But a thing exists because God knows it. We desire an object that exists. An object exists because God desires it. As the medieval thinkers put it: 'Scientia Dei causa rerum. Amor Dei causa rerum.' The knowing of God is the cause of things. The loving of God is the cause of things.

With reference to the fourth paragraph in this chapter, the sudden sense of a desire for no specific object is in fact the hallmark of a mystical experience. The most explicit and exciting description of this experience is C. S. Lewis's account of it in his autobiography, *Surprised by Joy* (pp. 16 and 72).

God could be defined – or rather pointed to – by this experience, as that which alone directly arouses my self-awareness as desirable; that which, not as object desired but as subject making desirable, causes in us that desire for we know not what which is the foundational religious experience.

This is why a religious conversion is always prefaced with a vague dissatisfaction with everything and a yearning for we know not what. This yearning is the symptom of a person's awakening at a deeper level; at the level where you are you and only that which *wants* you can move you.

This deeper level, and its privileged connection with the ultimate reality, is pointed to by Dag Hammarskjöld in *Markings* (p. 169):

I don't know who – or what – put the question, I don't know when it was put. I don't even remember answering. But at some moment I did answer Yes to someone – or something – and from that hour I was certain that existence is meaningful and that, therefore, my life, in self-surrender, had a goal.

12.

The second quadrant

In this quadrant, we enter the sphere of mystery, of the transcendent. I take as my starting-point a quotation from *The Heart of Philosophy* by Jacob Needleman.

> There was one experience of a certain kind that only much later in my life did I understand. I remember it down to the smallest detail. I had just turned fourteen. It was a bright October afternoon and I was walking home from school. I remember the trees and the coloured leaves underfoot. My thoughts were wandering when suddenly my name, 'Jerry', said itself in my mind. I stopped in my tracks. I whispered to myself: 'I am.' It was astonishing. 'I exist.' I began to walk again, but very slowly. And my existence was walking with me, inside me. I am fourteen years old and I am.
>
> And that is all. I did not speak about this experience to anyone, and for no other reason than that I gradually forgot about it. I went on reading every kind of book about the mind, nature, science; about philosophy; I read great novels. I plunged into classical music. But not once did anything I read, nor anyone or anything I heard, make mention, even remotely, of such an experience. Nothing in my environment or education reminded me of it. How could that be? What is culture, what is education, if it makes no place for that? And further, what is the right way of supporting that experience without spoiling it even more by the wrong kind of talk?

We have seen that desiring another person causes an arousal of the sense of myself as a person. Now what Needleman is talking about is an experience in which arousal is *not* by desiring another person but *from within myself.* But this self-awakening, although it is not *caused* by desire, is certainly not *without* desire. On the contrary, those who break this new level of awareness speak of a great 'longing' that comes with it. So what we have here is the reverse of the normal order in which desire for another awakes me to myself. Here the awaking to myself causes desire, a desire for I know not what, which we call 'longing'. The German for this is 'Sehnsucht', a very important word in German literature.

This is the most revealing experience that we have: a sense that I am *in myself* and not relatively to other people and to my culture and race, carrying with it a longing for I know not what. It is a sense of luminous identity generating desire.

What could be the object of this desire? It is nothing in particular. It cannot be named or categorized. It is, rather, a whole *world* in which I have significance, but not the way I am significant in *my* world of family, race, culture. Rather it is a world that is *giving* me my significance. Although Needleman does not make this explicit, this luminous sense of myself is a sense of myself as somehow chosen, of my personhood as a destiny. This sense of being chosen by some mystery altogether beyond the mind's reach is the break-through experience out of which the whole of the Jewish scripture grows. And the sense of my being significant as the result of a choice is the sense of my being desirable as the result of being desired. And that reality whose desiring *makes* desirable what it desires is the transcendent non-dependent reality we call God.

Thus the object of the 'longing' we are talking about is a reality that somehow 'desires' me, intends me. Now we have seen that all desire springs from the sense of being desirable and seeks the consummation of that sense in being desired. This longing, then, *is* a longing because it is looking to a mysterious one who desires me. In this longing, the sense of myself as desirable, that dynamizes all my desiring, gets an inward hint of its mysterious source that, since it *makes* me desirable, will totally fulfil all the desires that stem from this sense of myself as desirable.

In other words, in this longing, celebrated by mystics, poets, prophets, we experience *all* our loving, all our erotic engagement with friends and lovers, *at its source*. The implications of this are enormous. It revolutionizes, turns upside-down, our understanding of religion. Look up any commentary on the Hebrew prophets. There you will certainly be told that 'the prophet compares the love of God for his people with the love of a bridegroom for his bride'. The supposition is that the bedrock reality, that which the prophet fundamentally has in mind, is the mutual love of man and woman, *to* which he is comparing the *less* known relationship between the

38

human spirit and God. Once you have a taste of the luminous self and its longing, you see that it's the other way round. The bedrock reality for the prophet, the fundamental thing he/she has in mind, is the grounding sense of the self-in-God, *from* which he is deriving the significance of the love between man and woman. He sees that relationship transfigured by a mysterious light that other people tend not to see. It is not that the love of God for his/her people is like the love between bridegroom and bride. It is that the love between bridegroom and bride is like the mysterious love the prophet feels in his/her heart. Prophets and mystics have, and call us to recognize in ourselves, a direct taste of what underlies all our erotic and social experience. They elucidate our experience of feeling desirable through desiring another, with their deeper experience, of feeling our desirableness directly, at its source. They elucidate the experience of knowing our beauty *indirectly* through desiring another, with the deeper and grounding experience of knowing our beauty *directly* in the sudden sense of luminosity, chosenness, destiny, call and mission. The Hebrew prophets always start by giving their credentials: in every case, an experience of the Needleman break-through. Without this, all that they have to say is mere pious exhortation, morality with God's presumed blessing.

This leads to a distinction between two sorts of religiousness that is, I believe, the most important distinction there is to be made in the matter of religion: between a *romantic* religiousness and a religiousness in touch with the *source* of romanticism, a *mystical* religiousness. The scripture commentator who talks of the prophet as comparing the love of God to the love between man and woman is expressing romantic religiousness. Most sermons are coming out of romantic religiousness. We were all brought up on romantic religiousness. For this type of religiousness, the experiential base is common consciousness, consciousness that has not broken the level of luminous self-hood, consciousness confined to the social level where we measure ourselves by each other. That is the reality, the known, the sure. Religious truth is got by spinning a web of specu-lation and beautiful thoughts out of and beyond this sure base. It's up in the air, controlled only by the person's fancy as he/she conjures up a God who is like Grandma but infinitely better. So it's romantic. It's building castles in Spain. Mystical religiousness is the reverse of this. Its religious thinking is not up in the air, romantic, moralistic pious guesswork whose only anchor is ordinary social consciousness, but is *deeper*, *more* real than ordinary consciousness, and able to illuminate ordinary consciousness from this deeper and surer level. The parables of Jesus are a perfect example of this. The often strange behaviour of the people in these stories mirrors a consciousness that feels the heart of reality.

Today we are experiencing the bankruptcy of romantic religiousness, the need of religion to rediscover its source in a luminous self-awareness. One sign of this crisis is that the level of luminous self-awareness is being discovered by people who profess no religious belief, at least no traditional religious belief. That's the way history works. When the people who ought to be onto something aren't, outsiders get onto it. It is embarrassing for the believer to be confronted with a non-believer who is in touch with the *area* where faith grows while the believer is not! And agnostics who are at this level show signs of spiritual growth that are, too often, sadly lacking in believers.

This raises an important question. Let us use the word 'spirituality' to connote this area, this level of awareness, of what I have called the luminous self. The question is: What is the relationship between spirituality and religious faith? Spirituality is nearly indispensable to a live faith, but they are not the same thing. To equate them would be like equating physical fitness with e.g. winning a gold medal—that is, with what a person might *do* with physical fitness. Faith is a personal and free response to the situation revealed in spirituality. That situation, we have seen, is a sudden sense that 'I am', coupled with a longing for I know not what. Now this situation is one of great freedom. I am liberated from the constraints of purely social self-valuation, to live in an infinitely more spacious world. And I may simply *enjoy* this situation and use the many available meditation techniques to develop in it. But I may interpret this situation religiously. I may say 'Yes' to whatever it is that is 'choosing' me, and to the longing that I feel. I may allow my longing to become consent to the mysterious 'call' or 'choosing' or 'destining'. In any relationship, love is desire decided for, and this applies here. When a person makes this response, what we have is religious faith.

Faith, then, is not a leap in the dark, a blind act of mindless trust. It is not a guess, or the placing of a bet, as Pascal thought. It is not a decision to look at the universe in a certain way, or to enter a certain way of talking or 'language game'. People reach these truncated notions of what faith is because they don't have the above spiritual sense of themselves, so don't know the situation *of* which faith is the interpretation, *in* which faith works. All they have is the world the way it looks before a person wakes to him/herself; and in terms of that dull world they try to find a way of assenting to God, to the mystery that is the reason why the world is *not* dull. How can a person, living in a dead world, assent to a God who is the *vibrancy* of the world, in which the person does not believe? What I have called romantic religiousness is a good example of religiousness without spirituality, a religiousness that has to invent an exciting God to escape from the boredom of living in an unspiritual universe. Fundamentalism, so prevalent today, is another form of the same imbalance. It is an act of blind belief that escapes from a world and a selfhood *not* believed in. If you don't believe in yourself as a flaming miracle, how can you believe in God—except in a way that is going to make you and everyone else even more miserable? Alas, history furnishes many examples of this kind of religiousness.

Once the act of assent is made, the world does look different. The awakening to self as spirit is an enormous advance on the previous customary world-look; and the assent of faith is, in its turn, a huge advance on the realization of the world of spirit. The mystery to which I have surrendered returns the compliment, as it were, and gives signs of its presence and love. Sacraments begin to 'work'. Bernard Lonergan S.J., the most seminal theological thinker of our time, defines faith as 'the knowledge generated by religious love'. Religious love is that 'yes' I spoke of.

I have used the Needleman experience to introduce the vital idea of awareness of self as spirit. But it would be a mistake to suppose that until one has had an experience of this kind one has no such awareness. There are many ways to draw close to the deeper self-awareness. Here's a great description from *Zen and the Art of Motorcycle Maintenance* by Robert M. Pirsig:

To the untrained eye ego-climbing and selfless climbing may appear identical. Both kinds of climbers place one foot in front of the other. Both breathe in and out at the same rate. Both stop when tired. Both go forward when rested. But what a difference! The ego-climber is like an instrument that's out of adjustment. He puts his foot down an instant too soon or too late. He's likely to miss a beautiful passage of sunlight through the trees. He goes on when the sloppiness of his step shows he's tired. He rests at odd times. He looks up the trail trying to see what's ahead even when he knows what's ahead because he just looked a second before. He goes too fast or too slow for the conditions and when he talks his talk is forever about somewhere else, something else. He's here but he's not here. He rejects the here, is unhappy with it, wants to be farther up the trail but when he gets there will be just as unhappy because then the *it* will be 'here'. What he is looking for, what he wants, is all around him, but he doesn't want that because it *is* all around him. Every step's an effort both physically and spiritually because he imagines his goal to be external and distant. (p. 211)

We can all recognize ourselves in that portrait. I am trying to cure myself of ego-swimming, anxiously counting the laps and so forth.

Then there is Transcendental Meditation, currently used by millions of people. Give yourself ten minutes to start with. Sit on a hard chair (unless you are really comfortable cross-legged), erect but relaxed but erect but relaxed. Eyes shut, feet flat. According to the Dalai Lama, it is important for the thighs to be below the solar plexus—God knows why, and presumably the Dalai Lama. Let the mind empty out—it won't of course, but don't *hold onto* anything. Attend—but not closely—to your breathing, which should be from the abdomen. The moment you find your mind wandering or going after a thought, repeat some word or phrase (called a mantra) just to flick it back onto—nothing in particular. That sounds nonsensical, but with a little practice you will find in yourself a certain *aptitude* for inattention to particulars, for resting in nothing in particular. This aptitude is the key to spiritual awareness. Its discovery goes back to the dawn of history and is one of the most important discoveries about ourselves that we have ever made.

Now what I have just described is not a religious exercise, but it *is* a spiritual exercise. It easily becomes a religious exercise, and when it does so you have a form of prayer which totally transforms religious belief, gets you on the inside of the images in which belief is expressed. It does so when the *intention* of that word or phrase is to say yes to the all-embracing mystery, and when the *centering* on nothing in particular becomes the 'longing' for nothing in particular, a longing to which you are saying yes.

When a person's religious belief moves from its conventional, taught habitat into the habitat of centering prayer as described in the last paragraph, you have the transition from romantic to

42

mystical religiousness, which is the nerve of becoming religiously adult.

Re-read Needleman, and notice how amazed he was to find that nothing—but nothing—he came across in the course of a rich and sophisticated education made reference to the sort of experience that he had had and that he just knew was the most important thing that could happen to anyone. The reason for this systematic inattention to self as unique will become clear when we come to the third quadrant. There we shall analyse the enormously powerful, socially and culturally induced inertial tendency to stay with the self-awareness that we first learned, that consists in assessing ourselves in relation to others.

Add to this *universal* preference for the socio-culturally acquired over the quiet prompting of the spirit in us the enormous bias of our *scientific-technological* culture against what cannot be measured and bought and sold, and you will expect the resistance to spirit to be overwhelming. The odd thing is that spiritual awakening is commoner today than ever before. The reason is, surely, that our age has developed the one-sided materialistic side of ourselves to such an extent that the imbalance is no longer bearable, and the top-heavy, head-heavy structure begins to stagger. A time of socio-cultural bankruptcy is sometimes a time of spiritual awakening.

One idea keys this quadrant: an awareness of the self as luminous, as unique, as existing not in function of others but absolutely, as disturbingly free and responsible, as uniquely chosen, as longing for we know not what. This deeper level of consciousness is characterized by a reversal of the normal order of self-awakening, in which I feel myself as desirable and significant in desiring another. In the reversed order, self-awakening comes first and desire follows from it, and desire has no particular object since no particular object has aroused it but rather its very centre has stirred—as when a river ceases to follow its customary course and overflows its banks owing to a new pressure from its place of rising high up in the mountains.

This deeper self-awareness is where religious faith can take its rise. It meets formidable resistance in influencing and shaping human life, as we shall see in the third quadrant. The overpowering of that immemorial resistance by a new, sinless humanity, will be the theme of quadrant four.

13.

On the philosophic map (2)

To establish a sort of grammar of desire, here are five 'theses' to start with.

1. Created by desire, I am desirable. This is the basic truth, whose meaning however will not immediately appear.

2. Desirable, I desire; my pleasure in myself wants to extend itself to another. Desire, in other words, does not come out of emptiness but out of fullness.

3. Since it is out of desirableness that I desire, another who causes desire in me is touching my desirableness. To cause desire is to arouse desirableness.

4. It is my desirableness, thus aroused by another, that makes me want to *be* desired by that other.

5. Thus the vital centre of human relations is arousal; the awakening of a person's sense of being desirable, not (as commonly supposed) by being *desired* by another, but by being *aroused* by another *to* desire.

With this grammar as our working tool, we proceed to consider the crucial difference between the way God arouses a person and the way another person does. What is this difference? I suggest the following.

In both cases, the other awakens my sense of being desirable; but whereas the human other awakens my sense of being desirable *indirectly* through arousing the desire that stems from this sense, God touches my sense of being desirable *directly*, God's desire for me being what *makes* me desirable. Another way of putting this difference would be to say that the other excites my sense of being desirable retroactively, by starting-up what *stems* from this sense – in the manner, incidentally, that all virtues are acquired: by doing repeatedly the type of action that stems from a certain feeling, I encourage the feeling to awaken. There is a whole book on self-affirmation based on this very traditional idea, *Self-affirmation* by

George Weinberg. God's touch, on the other hand, does not work retroactively on the source of desire, but touches the source directly.

Thus in our interpersonal relations, desire for another points inward to the sense of being desirable, whereas the touch of God directly enlivens this sense so that there flows from it a strange, poignant, bittersweet (C. S. Lewis) desire for we know not what. In the one case, the movement is from desire to the desiring as desirable, in the other case it is from the desirable to desiring.

Now what is going to happen to our understanding of God's love for us if this basic grammar of desire is not mastered – specifically if it is not understood that it is by arousal and not by being desired that our basic sense of being desirable is quickened?

The basic thing we know from the gospel is that God loved us first. This is formally stated by John (1 John 4:10), and it is clearly fundamental to the whole gospel message. But because the subtle fact of awakening by being aroused rather than by being desired is not noticed, we have slipped into a way of thinking of people as awakening people by loving them rather than by 'turning them on' – so that when God enters the scene he becomes the supreme instance of this 'loving the person first', of this being my lover before I am the person's lover. So the mistake that we make between ourselves, of not understanding that people 'turn each other on' and *thus* awaken each other, gets magnified to infinity in our thinking about *God's* love.

More practically put, the statement that God loved us first easily evokes an experience of being loved first by another person in whom we are not interested – which is one of the most negative experiences we have. If there is nothing I want more than to be desired by one who arouses desire in me, there is nothing I want less than to be desired by one who does not excite me. It is surely a grave mistake to take this latter experience as our paradigm, thus creating the image of God as the forlorn, neglected lover, the eternal bore.

No, God is not the infinite exemplar of unrequited love. God's is the love that, utterly surprisingly, creeps up *on the inside* of our sense of ourselves as desirable which normally is awakened *from the outside* by the person who excites our longing. It is in that absolutely radical sense, that metaphysically imposed sense, that God 'loves us first'. God's loving, God's desire, makes us *to be* desirable, causes in us that sense of unique worth that dynamizes all that people do and want to do.

What we call grace, or the new creation, is that movement within

45

people whereby the infinite desire which constitutes them in being (the 'first creation') *happens for them*, happens in their consciousness, happens as a new empowering of the heart.

God has direct access to that in me which the beauty of another, and of all this world, of art, of music, of dance, arouses. It is the creator touch, the felt presence of the desire whereby I am, am desirable, and hence desirous.

Finally, I suspect that much of the theology that opposes agape to eros is bedevilled by this misunderstanding; its agape is a love austerely separate from the dynamic of arousal and graciously alighting on the undeserving creature, instead of being the heart of that dynamic, as the great mystics have always understood. Not surprisingly, the theologians of agape versus eros do not like the mystical tradition. I am thinking especially of Anders Nygren.

And pastorally, surely, it is more important to excite people, to interest people, to draw people out, than to 'love' them, than to convey a feeling for them which is regardless of what they may feel. The moment we forget that the people with whom we interact are possessed of a sense of unique worth that is only awakened in desiring, a sense that the mysterious infinite can awaken directly *to* desiring, we are on the wrong track. Jesus, after all, did not go around 'loving' people. He attracted them. He allowed God to show him to people as his beloved, desirable because desired from all eternity. As each of us is.

The most important implication of this cluster of ideas is, however, yet to be stated. It concerns the unity among people, and peoples, in the Body of Christ. Let me try to spell this out.

As we have already seen, it is the sense of self as desirable in people that draws them together through the stages of intimacy. Desirable, I desire another and hope to be desired by the other. Desirable, the other arouses me. Then his/her desirability, aroused by mine, is appropriated by him/her and thrown joyfully into the relationship. Now what happens to this whole interplay of good-nesses when each is experiencing him/herself as desirable *because desired by the infinite*? There arises between people in this community of faith a bond of another order altogether, an ineffable yet simple and very concrete empathy. Sometimes I can discern, quite over and above and other than the space I make for God in my life, God making space for him/herself in me. And *then* I sense other people's God-space. It is a unity in another order, yet totally penetrating and transforming our customary order and unity. In the Spirit, when our spirit moves in it, we *know* that we are one, and know that unity is the definitive sign of the Spirit. So each one's felt desirableness, which is the principle of intimacy, becomes, when known as God-desiredness, the place of that Logos-unity in which the infinite knows us all. And since our unity and flourishing in the Spirit is the elevation by God of our sense of being desirable in revealing himself as its source, it will be seen what a disastrous mistake is made when, as happens regularly in the fundamentalist writings, the spiritual life is taken to be opposed to the psychology that promotes a good self-image. In reality, the poor self-image that this kind of spirituality promotes is the persistence of original sin against the transforming work of the Spirit.

Finally, it is interesting that Aquinas did not equate charity, our God-instilled love, with grace, as Scotus did. For Aquinas, grace was in 'the essence of the soul', charity in 'the will'. This distinction between the essence of the soul — for the mystical tradition 'the fine point of the soul', fundus animae — and the will, looks like the distinction I am implying between the radical sense of being desirable and the desiring that flows out of that sense. Aquinas performed for his time the act of introspection required to order properly our understanding of God's gracious action in us. This chapter suggests what is the requisite introspection for our time. It is the discovery that desire is the arousal of the desirable, and not the cry of the empty heart.

GETTING THE FEEL OF THE IDEA

God desires us before we desire God
because God's desire makes us desirable
which we must be in order to desire anything at all.

In the new creation, we feel the creative touch of God's desire
stirring us in our desirableness to desire nothing that can be
    named
until this nothing is named as the cause of our desire
which, being the cause of desire, is desirable.

Thus, through the slow skill of grace in nature,
the lover becomes the lovely.

In our experience of each other, on the other hand, the lovely
    comes first
seen with the eyes of arousal;

47

we do not awake to being loved
except by one who loving us makes us desirable and thus able to
   love
and touching us stirs our desirability to want without object
until at last the lover becomes the lovely.

Between ourselves our hope is that the lovely will become the
   lover,
but beyond ourselves the hope is that the lover will be revealed
   as lovely.

What is needed is a double exercise in correction:
we have to correct the common way of thinking of how one person
   brings another along
in order to say that the revised version is how God does *not* bring
   us along!
We have to shift the emphasis from loving someone to arousing
   someone
in order to get a glimpse of one who has direct access to the
   aroused.

The relevant contrast is between direct access to our desirableness
and indirect access to it by alluring.
It is not the contrast between a (divine) love that is irrespective
   of desirableness
and a (human) love that depends on the desirableness of the
   object.

And the key to the whole thing is to understand human love as
   dependent, radically, on the desirableness *of the subject*
who is the apple of God's eye.

14.

The paradox of consciousness

There are two different 'messages' each of us is getting from consciousness – two levels at which we are conscious. At one level the message is something like this: 'I am this body, and around me are bodies.' At the other level, it might be something like this: 'I am. Why?'

At level 2, I am involved in a limitless mystery. So there is, at this level, an insatiable desire for this mystery to disclose its meaning. And there is a sense that the meaning is trying to come through – through me. Ayn Rand points to the intense curiosity in the eyes of a child, and says, 'If you ever see an adult who looks out in that way, you are in the presence of a great man or woman.'

Most important, at level 2 there is no difference between *the world* as order out of chaos and *my mind* as seeking this order. I am part of a mystery or order out of chaos, of light out of darkness.

None of these statements of the second level is satisfactory. Nor does this greatly matter. The point is, that we *have* this level where the huge sense of everything fills us. At this level, the world and I are one process of order coming out of chaos, light out of darkness.

Now these two levels are dramatically different. The first level is entirely practical, although it contains a lot of unnoticed metaphor and poetry for which it depends on level 2. Consider for instance the ancient habit, now taken for granted, of referring to the stars as heavenly *bodies*, and the formulation of physics that 'a body will continue in its state of rest, etc.' The model is *my* body. On this model, *everything* 'out there' is regarded as a body, having the sort of unity-in-multiplicity that my body has. In other words, there is a body-centred, a level-1 understanding of order-out-of-chaos as well as the level-2 sense of order-out-of-chaos. They mustn't be confused. But they always are.

Now the simplest way in which the two levels work together is as follows. The fundamental sense of order in the world comes from level 2, but the order is spelled out as a patterning *of the bodies* that form the staple diet of level-1 thinking. This simple arrangement comes into crisis when, for various reasons, the deep sense for order stirs anew, and demands a reordering of 'the bodies' (for instance, the flat earth gives way to a sphere on which we are walking) even to the point of becoming dissatisfied with the very *notion* of bodies – as with quantum mechanics.

Thus level 1, or common sense, never has the last word. What calls the shots is the insatiable and mysterious thrust toward the light – level 2. But, as we have looked at the matter so far, they work together.

But when someone asks a really fundamental question and means it – for instance, 'Is there God? Does our life have any ultimate meaning or purpose?' – that is a stirring at level 2 that *cannot* be spelled out at level 1 – except in poetry or prophecy. *But people never realize this.* They try to think out their wondering in the only way they know how, that is, 'in bodies'. So when they think about 'the ultimate reality', or 'God', they are thinking of this as somehow bodily – a very transparent kind of bodiliness, but 'out there', the way bodies are, because it's very hard not to. That's an experiment you can try. Try to think about, say, 'being', or 'God', or 'consciousness', and you'll find yourself *imagining something* that in some way 'does for' the thing you're thinking about. Lonergan points out that it took even a great mind like Augustine twenty years, and it has taken science about four centuries, to discover that 'reality' does not mean the same thing as 'body'.

You have an exceptionally crude example of this mistake in the statement of a Soviet astronaut, that he had found no God 'out there'. It is interesting to compare this with the profoundly religious reaction of some of the American astronauts when they contemplated earth from lunar space. That was a very different mental process, not merely a *statement* the opposite of the Soviet's. The men were so overwhelmed by what they saw – which technology had brought within their reach, basic level-1 stuff – that *their level 2* was stirred, and *they spoke out of that sense of wonder.* They spoke on the intercom the words of Genesis 1 which, incidentally, is a marvellous piece of level-2 thinking, its two intertwining motions of animation ('the spirit of God moved over the waters') and verbalization ('God said "Light be!" and light became.') which, we have already seen, is how people come into intimacy.

We can further sketch in the features of the two levels by

considering *thinking* and *insight*. Thinking is basically mechanical – we can say that it 'arranges the bodies' according to the pattern given it to work with. But the pattern itself comes from insight, which is a level-2 event. Certainly the sense for order that seeks the pattern is at level 2.

This analysis enables us to deal with the question, 'Do computers think?' They do. Thinking is a mechanical process, and computers can do it for us – and much more efficiently. A computer can work through centuries of calculation in a few hours. But no computer, however sophisticated they may become, will ever have an insight. For an insight – whether of Newton or Einstein or you when you first understood something – is a successful stirring of wonder that *you are* (level 2).

Another question can be resolved. It is often asked: Is the order in the universe 'really out there', really *in* the things, or is it only in our minds? Answer: neither. The question is a false one. For consciousness at level 2 does not know the distinction between world-order and mind-order. At that level, I am bathed in the original mystery of order coming out of chaos. My mind, as I try to work out the world order, is part of the very process of world order, *is* the world order as mind. The new scientists are coming to understand this participation of the mind in the world it is studying: and it will be the greatest revolution science has ever known.

But our culture in its mainstream as represented by the academic world has no place for level 2. It recognizes no self bathed in mystery, no self that is partner to everything in a single mystery of structured emergence. Its 'self' is a level-1 self – a body surrounded by bodies and considering all the complex relations between them.

The starvation – nay the strangulation – caused by this confinement is evident in the desperate reactions it provokes: fundamentalism, the multiple cults of our time, the drug scene. These are bizarre expressions of level 2, just as repressed sexuality will try to 'get back' in bizarre ways.

In short: There is the self that fits, and the self that is part of the original scheme of things: the self that gets its meaning and role from others, and the self that is *in* the meaning, of itself and of others; the self that is now and the self that was always.

Here is this idea, in the more technical philosophical language of Eric Voegelin:

There is the paradoxical structure of consciousness. On the one

51

hand, we speak of consciousness as a something located in human beings in their bodily existence. In relation to this concretely embodied consciousness, reality assumes the position of an object intended. Moreover, by its position as an object intended by a consciousness that is bodily located, reality itself acquires a metaphorical touch of external thingness. We use this metaphor in such phrases as being conscious of something . . . I shall call this structure of consciousness its intentionality, and the corresponding structure of reality its thingness. On the other hand, we know the bodily located consciousness to be also real; and this concretely located consciousness does not belong to another genus of reality, but is part of the same reality that has moved, in its relation to man's consciousness, into the position of a thing-reality. In this second sense, then, reality is not an object of consciousness but the something in which consciousness occurs as an event of participation between partners in the community of being. (from *Order in History*, vol. 5)

Now we can deduce from a belief that God is, that we only are because God desires us, that our being is good and desirable because we are absolutely and mysteriously desired. But can we point to any *experience* of this fundamental truth about ourselves? Not if we remain confined, in our sense of what is real and really counts, to the practical level where consciousness is showing to each of us only 'this body surrounded by bodies'. Until the *mystery* of being conscious suggests itself, talk of a mysterious desiring Other is vacuous. It is precisely this imbalance between an inner imperviousness to mystery, on the one hand, and enthusiastic God-talk on the other, that is the hollow note in fundamentalist preaching.

Prayer is the taking quite seriously of myself-as-mystery. It is the kind of fumbling that takes place when I try to *stay* with this sense of myself. For St John of the Cross and the central Catholic mystical tradition finely represented in our time by Abbot Chapman, the growth crisis that inaugurates contemplative prayer is the point where cherished methods break down and there is only fumbling – what Chapman calls 'an idiotic state'. St John and St Teresa knew well the danger that this floundering condition would be interpreted as spiritual collapse, and that the inability to do anything else would lead to giving up prayer altogether.

They were speaking out of a culture very different than ours. For them, the solid world that the person at this stage was being called to go beyond was a religious world, a culture whose settled world-view was religiously, not scientifically, shaped. Hence they could lay great stress on the importance of having had religious satisfaction at the earlier, pre-contemplative stage. Something must *have* worked for its breakdown to *be* a breakdown. One must not enter prematurely on the prayer of fumbling. But what about our world, in which the immemorial bias toward the practical has not been allowed to take a religious shape. For us there *is* no immature, culture-supported religiousness. We may expect, then, that our first real religious experience will be the fumbling experience, a new sense of myself already publicly acknowledged and universally shared to give way to a new and mystifying way of praying. For us, it is a question of allowing a systematic and universal blindness to give way to 'what I have always known I wanted', as Harry says in T. S. Eliot's play, *The Family Reunion*. There is a profound difference between the concealment of the mystical sense under a powerful religious culture, and its repression under the dictates of a scientific culture.

Our culture has in it a systematic reluctance to let the mystery of being conscious suggest itself. We inhabit a scientific culture; and a scientific culture – as opposed to the open-ended desire-to-know which drives science itself – is one in which the results of scientific exploration at the practical level are what count in the fashioning of our common mind.

Now it seems to me that the scientific culture bias will give way more easily to the emergent mystical sense than would the old religious culture. For the modern bias is *simply* repressive of the mystical, whereas a religious culture half-accepts the mystical. Thus in a religious culture the mystical sense has a safety-valve, so that the crisis over allowing the full and direct force of the spirit to come into play tends to be postponed. The scientific culture, on the other hand, imposes on its participants the alternatives of remaining spiritually asleep or waking up. And the awakening, here, will be an awakening to *all* that the culture represses: the infinite value of the self, and its crucifixion by the culture in the affluent and in the deprived world. Unlike the birth of contemplative prayer in the medieval monastery, its birth today will be political, and generate a holy rage against the suicidal policies of our time. If we will let it.

The Christian mystical tradition insists that authentic contemplative experience has an affective dimension. Very obscurely, with no

53

clear object, there is a movement of the heart; for this guarantees that what we have is not just an inner peace in ourselves but a relationship with an other. I suspect that the awakening of the real self from its sleep in modern culture has about it an element of relief that is already a kind of loving. The contrast between the practical world of 'normal' modern awareness and the world that can awake in us is, precisely, the difference between an essentially lonely-with-palliatives and a participatory existence. And to feel with relief the end of loneliness, however confusingly, is to feel in love.

15.

Four openings of desire to its ultimate cause

I discern four ways in which desire opens itself to the ultimate cause of desire.

1. Through an intimate relationship. Interdependence, unlike dependence, is unpredictable. And desire launched on the unpredictable is headed for the ultimate mystery of desire. A deep relationship makes you wonder what you want from life.

2. Through the extension of intimacy, after the manner of Leo Buscaglia, to many people, especially to those disturbingly unlike ourselves in culture, etc. The basis of Buscaglia's thought is this fact: the way to extend intimacy is to *take initiatives* with people, to *approach* the stranger. What deters us from doing this is a poor self-image and consequent expectation of rejection. What motivates us to take these initiatives is a *good* (that is, a true) sense of ourselves, which is the basis of my whole theology. In the wider pursuit of intimacy, also, we meet the unpredictable; and, as in (1), desire feeling the unpredictable is desire headed for the ultimate mystery of desire. ('The ultimate mystery of desire', 'what desire is all about', 'the ultimate cause of desire' – all these phrases refer to the same reality.)

3. Through creative solitude and inner silence, meditation and centring prayer, we learn a capacity in ourselves for attending to what seems to be nothing but is really the nothing-in-particular which is God. Centring prayer is a technique for giving breathing-space to a desire in us for we know not what, which is the cause of desire.

4. Through conscience. Conscience is the drawing of desire by something *different* from my obvious betterment, and often opposed to it. It is the feeling of desire *as* my impulse toward a fuller, less self-centred life. And thus it is an important example of that arousal of desire which does not come from a particular object but, if you

like, from what desire is really all about, namely the journey toward life's goal. Choosing a career, I might wonder, 'Yes, but what is a career like that going to make of *me*? What sort of person is it going to turn me into? Do I like that person?'

But conscience tends to work in an indirect way. We feel its tug only when we are embarked on a *bad* way, and so we tend to mistake its true significance, getting it all snarled up in guilt. We experience conscience as the counterpull. It isn't easy to recognize that it is conscience that is the pull, the way it warns us off the counterpull. One of the most exciting moments in all philosophical history is when Socrates, on trial for his life, tells his judges that he has an inner 'daimon' or spirit, that guides him. But, he explains, his daimon only warns him when he is taking the wrong way, it does not tell him the right way. Then comes the great moment. This morning, he says, as I set out for this court and certain death, my daimon did not deter me.

None of these four ways is exclusive of the others. On the contrary they interact – unpredictably! They are really only aspects of a conspiracy, on the part of the cause of all our desiring, to awaken us to itself, to bring about the generic arousal which hopes for an ultimate intimacy, for intersubjectivity with the infinite.

Although the third way is followed in solitude, it brings more and more into awareness a self that is all people, the Christ self. There is a reason for this. To feel the desire that motivates all my living, to feel my essential nerve of desire, is to feel the desire that motivates all people. The nerve of all my life runs through all the living. The mystic is one who is learning *the sense* in which 'we are all one person', to quote the young Freeman Dyson.

If I am asked to set all this in context of our historic present, I would say: We are rediscovering the real human being. The real human being is being-in-desire, and desire looks for its fulfilment to the cause of desire which, revealing itself as desirous, admits to intimacy, the peace beyond understanding.

16.

Hope is desire in the skilled hands of God

We just explored four 'openings' of desire to the pull of the mystery of our existence as desirous beings: an intimate relationship, the expansion of intimacy to an every-widening circle, centring prayer, and the tug of conscience. There is a common element to these four 'openings'. Each of them is a process whereby desire is detached from a definite, specific object (e.g. this person as dependable upon for strokes, etc.) and launched into an unpredictable future (e.g. the way our relationship might go, or the surprises I shall meet in a life of expanded intimacy). In this new situation of unpredictability, desire becomes hope. And to hope is to be drawn by a future to which I feel positively. It is to be *drawn* by the future as opposed to merely *moving* into the future.

A thing to notice about this 'drawing' phenomenon is that that which *is drawing* is unknown (as opposed to the definite object drawing desire), *and* that that which *is drawn* in me is much more 'me' than is the initial attraction to the definite object. It is not so much *my desire* as *my desirousness*, my investment in life itself, that is being drawn. And so my desirousness, my being-in-desire, is being drawn by something unknown. To this unknown attracting force, not just my desire but my very *capacity* to desire, my very hopefulness as a desiring being, responds. Thus as desire responds to the particular object that causes it, desirousness, awakened in hope, responds to the unknown reality that causes *it*.

Very briefly, desire matures into hope, and hope is being drawn into the unpredictable future by the unknown cause of desire.

Gabriel Marcel wrote a fine book thirty or so years back entitled *Homo Viator*, man the wayfarer. It was a profound analysis of the sorely neglected virtue of hope. He made one serious mistake, however, which was to *contrast* hope with desire, saying that hope was one thing, desire quite another. This is like saying an oak is one thing, an acorn quite another. In reality, hope *is* desire in

57

the skilled hands of God. Hope *is* desire, learning its fundamental meaning, its orientation toward the alluring cause of desire – *with* which, ultimately, it seeks intimacy, which is the peace that passes all understanding.

Eliot expresses superbly this being drawn, by the origin of all desire ('where we started') to explore and thus come home:

> With the drawing of this Love and the voice of this Calling

> We shall not cease from exploration
> And the end of all our exploring
> Will be to arrive where we started
> And know the place for the first time.
> Through the unknown, remembered gate
> When the last of earth left to discover
> Is that which was the beginning;
> At the source of the longest river
> The voice of the hidden waterfall
> And the children in the apple-tree
> Not known, because not looked for
> But heard, half-heard, in the stillness
> Between two waves of the sea.

('Little Gidding' – 5)

17.

The radical discontinuity

Jacob Needleman says something in *The Heart of Philosophy* that I had let slip when I first read it, for it was so jagged and unrelatable to my work. Describing a boy in his class suddenly awakening to the question 'Why do I exist?' as a personal question, he says that the eyes lit up in a strange way, and that the question thus experienced had nothing to do with anything else. Here is what Needleman says:

> As I launched into my answer to Eric and as I excitedly began making new connections between ideas, I caught a glimpse of his eyes. I was stunned. My God, there was a person there in those eyes. And I was not speaking to that person, or to any person.
>
> I was suspended between seeing the person and being drawn into ideas. It was a moment of great intensity, great reality. Somewhere, somehow, I understood this moment and was grateful for it. I saw that I was in fact in between two movements in myself, two major aspects of my own being. In short, I myself was in question. I saw that these two movements had no relationship to each other.

I let this observation pass me by. It was only later that it hit me: 'It's true!' We exist in two worlds that have absolutely nothing to do with each other. *That* world is its own. It is discontinuous with *this*. Until I recognize this, my eyes are shut.

But surely, it will be argued, my experience in both worlds is itself the continuity between them. Yes, my experience is the continuity, but only as experiencing, suffering, the discontinuity.

My inauthentic existence, on the other hand, disguises the discontinuity. I can look back on a long life and see myself as ground between these two worlds that have nothing to do with each other. I dealt with the experience by 'leaking' that world into this, where it shows up in inflated relationships and an inflated idea of myself. That world, leaked into this, distorts it, breeds what Eliot calls 'unreal emotions, and real appetite'. Conversely there is the tendency in my writing and teaching to sell the other world short, to make it folksy with the warmth of this world.

The discontinuity has not to be 'handled', cleared up, resolved. It has to be lived, and, when lived, then it transforms. It should not surprise us – though I have only just come to this insight – that Eliot gives the discontinuity as that which requires sanctity and gives to sanctity its definition. I have only just come to understand these lines:

> Men's curiosity searches past and future
> And clings to that dimension. But to apprehend
> The point of intersection of the timeless
> With time, is an occupation for the saint –
> No occupation either, but something given
> And taken, in a lifetime's death in love,
> Ardour and selflessness and self-surrender.

> ('The Dry Salvages' 5)

Why, I wondered, the heavy, reiterative emphasis, the catalogue of required virtues hardly making for poetic elegance? The answer is that to accept, with the docility appropriate to each, the grinding of the two bewilderingly different worlds, is *the* work of a lifetime, the work of life, and making of holiness or wholeness.

What is slowly learned from the work is what is the true nature of the discontinuity. The other world disturbs most in the sudden dispositions and requirements it makes *for this world*. It is *not* alien to this world, we come to learn. It is intimate to it – but on its own quite incomprehensible terms.

How indispensable to any right understanding of this matter is a true idea of consciousness! Consciousness is not what I know. It is I, knowing, experiencing, suffering, delighting, accepting. Consciousness is the humility of experience. It is the capacity *to be*, without explanation or reassuring soliloquy, in eternity and in filling-in the forms of time.

As the rugged discontinuity of the two worlds requires, and defines, holiness, says what is the 'whole' of holiness, so it is this discontinuity that requires, and defines, the great atoning act of God in Christ. So a few lines later Eliot says:

60

These are only hints and guesses,
Hints followed by guesses; and the rest
Is prayer, observance, discipline, thought and action.
The hint half guessed, the gift half understood, is Incarnation.
Here the impossible union
Of spheres of existence is actual,
Here the past and future
Are conquered, and reconciled,
Where action were otherwise movement
Of that which is only moved
And has in it no source of movement –
Driven by daemonic, chthonic
Powers.

At different times of my life I have had different interpretations of those 'spheres of existence'. Now at last I am in no doubt – in other words I never really understood that line before. They are the two discontinuous worlds we live in. There union *is* impossible: yet in the new life in Christ it is actual. It is brought about by the four-stage process of transformation of desire: (1) the stretching of desire by Jesus to the objectless infinity of *the other world*; (2) the concentration of this liberated desire in a symbol *in this world*: Jesus; (3) desire deprived of this object: the crucifixion and death of Jesus; (4) the sign and taste of the world to come: the encounter with the risen Jesus and the inebriation with Holy Spirit. It is through this process of Incarnation that time is 'conquered and reconciled', so that we are no longer projected out of an unknown past into an unwilled future by 'daemonic, chthonic powers'. This will be our theme in the Fourth Quadrant.

To be awakened to, and co-operative with, the discontinuity, is to feel other people in a quite new and altogether more intimate way. For in laying-bare *to myself* my bewildered existence in this world, my forlornness, my defencelessness, I am laying myself bare to another and evoking in the other the same self-awakening. This solidarity among the truly solitary, this shared pathos of an existence that cannot account for itself, is the reason why the atonement breakthrough is social, sacramental, celebratory. I recall that in the early days after my awakening to the discontinuity in myself there was a rebirth in feeling, in compassion, of a kind that I have never had since with the same intensity, and to whose subsequent dimming I must attribute a dulling of the heavenly vision itself. For the capacity to feel must be locked up in this primal sense of lostness, wonder, and desire. If there is a reason why I exist, to what awesomely unknown will am I responsible and, unknowingly, responding? No human feeling – even the most bizarre and violent, nay especially these – but would be thus responsive. Why are there saints and criminals? Whence is 'the boredom and the horror and the glory' – Eliot's triad? Perhaps there is a notion of God that lies at the root of all false notions of God and consequently of the self. It is the notion of an all-knowing one whose serene omniscience would float above our self-aware existence and leave no trace in it. If God is not pressing on me to know myself, God does not know me.

18.

The indefiniteness of God language

A question that is always asked, at the point in my theology course where I try to show where and how our spiritual structure is open to God, is 'But where does *God* come in?' People seem to experience a frustrating vagueness at this point.

The following is an attempt to account for this by examining the *conditions* for thinking about God when one believes in God.

The believer who starts to think about the God in whom he/she believes very soon runs into the following problem. On the one hand, God is, for me as believer, very real, indeed the supreme reality, the most real. On the other hand, God is infinite or – same word – non-definite. No concept, no idea, no image, captures this supreme reality. So God is nothing that I can point to or fix my mind on. Now this means that God does not have the *kind* of reality that normally grabs the mind *because it is there*, like the planet Mars or my kidneys. For everything except God, there has to be evidence for asserting its existence, something we can look for in the world and, not finding it, we have to say that we have no grounds for the assertion. God does not present him/her/itself with this kind of compelling reality.

Understand me well. The point I am making is not that God is difficult to believe in because his reality cannot be proved. I am saying that the convinced believer finds God to be real all right but, being human, sometimes wishes that God's reality would impress itself on us the way other realities do.

If we look at the Hebrew Scriptures, we soon learn that believers have had this difficulty from the beginning. The people are continually turning to idolatry: that is, succumbing to the temptation to make God more available, to have something to show for our belief as our pagan neighbours do. The people who made a golden calf and declared 'Here is the God who brought us out of Egypt!' found

63

they could no longer stand the strain of worshipping an imageless, an unimaginable God.

The response of the prophets to this conduct was always the same. Do God's will, uphold the poor, the widow and the orphan, and God will become most real to you. A most precious wisdom is contained in this, that mystics have deepened and refined, namely: that the proper evidence for the reality of God is something that happens in the heart – and in the life – of one who *treats* God as real, who makes the often lonely choices for justice and compassion that this treating God as real demands. The person who surrenders his/her life to God's call will come to *know* God with a sureness surpassing all other knowing. For that person will come to know God *in the movement of her/his own heart* as it stretches out to God. The human heart moves out to God with a peacefulness and sureness that is not present in any other of its movements, and it is by this difference in the person that the difference between divine and finite reality is known.

So when we make a chart showing the structure of desire in a person, we cannot put God on that chart and we do not need to. All we have to show on the chart is desire behaving in a way that it only does when God is being experienced. This means that all that has to go on the chart is (a) the awakening of the sense of myself *not* consequent to a desire for a particular object, (b) the consequent movement of desire in all directions or without a particular object. Put God *on* the chart, and you have taken away from God her/his/its very essence, which is infinity, the peculiar capacity to be beyond everything and in everything that only God has, and that the faithful believer spends a lifetime discovering.

The believer has always to heed the warning: in your zeal to affirm that God is real, be careful not to make God limited. An example of this practical limiting of God is the creationists' reaction to evolution. They have got God so tied up with the *pictured, imagined* miracle of making the world in six days, that they have failed to see how much more powerfully the universe of contemporary science suggests the infinite mystery of God than does the old notion of the potter with his clay.

19.

Centring prayer

The simplest form of awakening to God is described by Needleman: a new, intense sense of self, accompanied with a desire for I know not what, a desire to do with the feeling of being a destiny.

This condition of being suddenly alive and wanting I know not what cannot be induced. It simply happens. But from time immemorial, in different cultures and religious climates, people have used a method for quieting or simplifying consciousness so that a person may be better *disposed* for the moment of awakening. Thus while the moment of awakening consists in *wanting* nothing in particular, the method consists in *thinking* of nothing in particular.

This sustained inattention to particulars has been found to be therapeutic. It is a step toward that 'inner freedom from the practical desire' of which Eliot speaks in 'Burnt Norton': a freedom of desire to move to I know not what as opposed to being pulled this way and that by definite objects. It creates a climate in which that simple wanting more easily makes itself felt. And when a person has already been able to identify a desire for God in her/himself, the method is an excellent way to let this desire affirm itself.

Here, briefly, is the method, already indicated on p. 42:

1. I sit, upright but relaxed, preferably in a chair of the bathroom or diningroom type – unless I can sit cross-legged without any strain or pain.

2. I spend a few moments letting the stuff in my mind empty itself out.

3. I try to maintain this simple, unconnected condition, but *not* by trying to stop thinking – that's impossible – but by just letting my thoughts happen without running after them. It takes a few times to learn this vital distinction between *following* my thoughts and *letting-be* my thoughts. I treat *sounds* that go on while I am meditating exactly as I treat my thoughts – let them go on, not trying to cut them out but remaining detached from them.

4. Whenever I find that I *have* been following a thought, I quietly *remind* myself of what I am doing by repeating a word or phrase that I find helpful. The 'mantra', as this is called, is not to be thought about, but to remind myself not to think with! It has been compared to a dummy put in the mouth of an infant (= the busy mind).

5. Breathing is important, but don't make a big deal of it. It will slow down of itself, and it should be centred on the abdomen, unlike the shallow breathing that accompanies anxiety.

6. After 15–20 minutes, I return to normal consciousness by saying the 'Our Father' or any other formula.

Basil Pennington has a useful classification of the type of thoughts that go through one's head. He lists five categories: (1) simple thoughts; (2) catching thoughts, the type that *want* you to follow them; (3) monitoring thoughts – 'Am I doing this right, am I wasting my time, what about my breathing, etc?'; (4) bright thoughts, brilliant ideas, insights; (5) stressful thoughts. Naming one's thoughts in this way is quite a good way of getting some distance from them. I have a mnemonic for this. Imagine the beach near the waterline where there is a scum forming. Imagine a bus moving along the line of the scum: a SCUM BUS.

The Third Quadrant

20.

Introducing the third quadrant

Now we have to play the whole tune again, in a different key.

The sense of being desirable, which grounds all our relating, whether 'to another, or to others, or to God', has a history, *is* a history. It gets off to a start that is the strangest thing about us, whose description taxes all the resources of language.

The infant is hedonic, swimming dolphin-like in a sea of delight. But the more this hedonic condition strives to become conscious, the more there enters a note of deprivation. This is something importantly different from Wordsworth's conception, of the child coming into this world 'trailing clouds of glory' and gradually succumbing to the dullness of our world. What Wordsworth implies is an early consciousness subsequently disappointed. In reality, it is the *coming* of consciousness that is at once the awakening to a limitless possibility and a withdrawal of that promised glory. The state of being 'in love with the world', that Margaret Mahler finds in the two-year-old, encounters perforce the mother's unresolved anxiety and, later, a blocking of the first enormous love for the mother by the presence of another and quite obscure claim on her, the father's.

Thus our sense of being desirable is, in historic generic genetic reality, a sense of glory not available, a sense of a hugeness of life possibility for which I am somehow disabled. But – and this is vital – the glory defines the disablement, says what the disablement is. When Paul asked the Lord to remove 'the thorn in his flesh' and heard 'my grace is sufficient for you', he was making a discovery that we still are far short of: that the weakness, the wonkiness, the wobble in one's life is due precisely to the glory's withdrawal and *therefore* is the place for grace's entry. 'Where I am weak, there am I strong.' The strength works in the weakness not primarily 'to stop us boasting' but because the strength is the secret, the ratio *of* the weakness.

69

In this third quadrant, I attempt to flesh out this strange, original condition of glory and deprivation. I do this in terms of the two great crises of infant life, the separation and the Oedipal crisis. I then try to set this process of rapid personal growth in the larger context, of us as an animal species becoming conscious.

21.

Two crises

In the first crisis encountered by the emerging self, we see the essential anguish and hope of our existence. For it is the crisis of my first realization that I am a separate, individual existence. The awfulness of this will not fully come home to me till much later when I face a fateful decision, but the feeling of it comes at age one to two.

Margaret Mahler, the brilliant pediatrician, has documented this crisis in *The Psychological Birth of the Human Infant*. She discerns four sub-phases of it: (1) at age one month or so, the first stirrings of an individual consciousness; (2) the 'practising' phase, the rapid acquisition of motor skills leading to the *practical* discovery 'I am, because I work, this works'. The third is the most important and is receiving much further study. It is the 'rapprochement' phase. In the exhilarating confidence induced by motor skills, etc., I return to mother for corroboration. As that most alarming thing, 'conscious separate existence', really gets under way, the need for support becomes enormous. And not for a support of the crutches type that would *mitigate* the venturesomeness of individual reality, but for a total *encouragement* in it. The first powerful sense of self looks ecstatically to the mother for support in an incredible adventure. This places on the mother a burden that no one can fully shoulder. She has to combine a pushing-away of the child with enormous emotional support. To the extent that she fails to sustain this ambiguity, the child receives the message: either be part of me, or be on your own. These alternatives are intolerable, and to the extent that the child gets this kind of message his first idea of how it feels to *be* 'I' is less than ecstatic.

We might see in this moment, of ecstatic expectation directed to the mother and disappointed into the normal anxious existence of the human animal, *the* human moment, in which we can read all the tragedies and glories of humankind.

71

Notice a most important thing about this 'less than ecstatic sense of being I'. It is not the feeling 'I'm not much good' but the feeling 'It's not all that good to be "I".' The importance of this is that our fundamental uncertainty touches not our *character* ('Am I a good person?'), as to which others could reassure us, but our very *existence*, which is beyond the reach of others, who in any case suffer the same radical uncertainty. Thus we get the hint, later to be expanded, that the *spiritual* self-awareness that opens us to the touch of the ultimate mystery, is thus opening us to a needed healing grace.

An equally important consequence of the separation-crisis and its less-than-happy outcome is this. Not having received from the mother a totally satisfactory send-off on life's journey, the person remains, to that extent, tied to the mother for the rest of his/her life. The unfinished business with the mother is never finished. The vague dread that everyone harbours at a deep level and which the healthy learn to deal with, is mother-referred. And this initial mother-referredness lays the foundation for all subsequent states of self-awareness, starts the habit of seeing one's life as not entirely satisfactory and looking to others for reassurance. In fact, we look to others for reassurance while it is the very investment of our self-esteem in others that is the cause of our not feeling too good about ourselves and so *needing* reassurance. This basic *habit* starts with the mother, the original 'other', and extends to all the people we interact with. The imperfectly separated individual existence looks continually to the other whence it has been unable clearly to pull away. Not knowing ourselves apart from others is our trouble, to remedy which we look to others!

Now this 'habit', of seeing myself in terms of others, of rating myself in the eyes of others, of measuring myself by others – this it is which so powerfully impedes the Needleman breakthrough into a luminous selfhood, the prophetic response to the call from the depths of existence which says, 'You are mine. You are not your family's, your class's, your race's, your party's. You are mine.' I call this habit the 'first focus' of consciousness. This first focus, in which self is all enmeshed with other, is influential over us without a rival. Why would anyone *think* of being him/herself other than the way they *first* came to consciousness? The world on which we first opened our eyes psychologically comes to be *the* world.

The original habit (and yes, we can think of 'original sin' in this connection) of self-assessment-by-others undergoes a crucial complexification at the second-of-all crisis, the Oedipal phase.

What happens at that stage is this. The child's immense love toward the mother, which emerged at the climax of the separation-crisis, now moves into very strange waters.

The love that the child has for the mother is sexually undifferentiated. It is very strong, because it is the first 'translation' of their original oneness into interpersonal feeling. In this huge tenderness, the child makes a total bid for the mother's affection. Freud says that this is the most powerful love we have ever experienced, though we have largely forgotten it. We have 'repressed' it – and R. D. Laing defines repression as 'forgetting something and forgetting you've forgotten it'.

This total claim on the mother encounters a mysterious rival, the father's claim. I use the word 'mysterious' advisedly. For a normal or straight rival is one who is after what I am after *in the way that I am after it*. But this other claimant on the mother is after what I am after but in a quite different way that I simply don't understand at all. The father is, at one and the same time, *another claimant* and *another kind of claimant*, and this is very difficult for the child to handle. Margaret Mahler says that we are still quite in the dark as to how the child feels about the intimate relationship between the parents.

The resolution of this collision that is not a straight collision is that this total claim on the mother becomes a no-no, and is repressed. Robert Stein, a maverick Freudian, maintains that our deepest trauma is that inflicted by this repression. He calls it the incest wound. I suspect that this is an important part of that repression of our sense of being desirable which is the root of our weakened relationship with God, people, and planet. The child's total zest for life, the sense of being welcome everywhere without strings attached, meets its first great disappointment in the mother's commitment to an 'other' in an 'other' way.

The *other side* of this repression of the original hedonism of the child, the pay-off, is a promotion to the status of the parents: one is male or female, as they are. It's the original version of 'If you can't beat 'em, join 'em!'

Now this is a huge step. The child has no hope of maintaining by him/herself this newfound sexual identity. He/she looks to the parents as models for it – the boy, to the father, the girl to the mother. The appropriate parent becomes my 'over-me' or 'Ueber-Ich' – Freud never used the abstract Latinism, 'superego': this has been left to his followers who, according to Bruno Bettelheim, bear much responsibility for the misunderstanding of Freud.

There it is in the barest outline: the id (total love-bid made a no-no and repressed), the ego (one's new identity as male or female) and the superego (the parental role-model reinforcing the repression). And the repressed total love is 'id'. What is interesting about this from a theological point of view is that it illustrates the manner in which evil comes on the scene. My total bid for love, stemming from my total desirability, which I have from God, becomes a no-no in the unavoidable drama where the two 'loves' collide. Thus repressed, it becomes a threat. Is this, then, all that evil is — what we make of ourselves in repressing our passionate nature? This is the view of a psychologist called Reich; he calls repression 'the murder of Christ'. Where this view is inadequate, I think, is that it fails to take into account the fact that *in* repressing our passionate nature we are discounting *our desirability*, which is our experience of ourselves as God's desired. Once *that* is understood, then certainly we can say that repression is the origin of evil, and that what our transformation will consist in is the final befriending of *all* that is in us that we have *had* to repress on our first steps into personhood. God is that infinite intelligence for which there is no such thing as evil. Evil arises out of self-doubt on the part of God's self-aware creatures. And the closer a person or a community comes to God, the more their 'dark side' becomes light.

What is happening at the Oedipal phase is that, on the one hand, there is a further repression of the infant's sense of being desirable (the first repression occurs with the imperfectly negotiated separation crisis) and, on the other hand, the habit of seeing oneself as a function of others is greatly strengthened: for now I am self-defined as 'boy' or 'girl' in the drama. At the dawn of the Oedipal phase, the child is beating at the doors of adulthood, determined to get in on the act, albeit an 'act' he/she does not understand. And, once in on the act, the child is further involved in the habit of seeing self as a function of others. Gender plays a crucial role in this habituation. The child does not grow up in a world of persons, but in a world of women and men, and is drawn progressively into that world with all its limiting of consciousness. And the long-forgotten sense that it should be blissful to be, gone underground with the separation crisis and driven deeper underground with the Oedipal crisis, is still down there, waiting to respond with passion when the deeper level of existence is broached and self-as-spirit is fledged.

74

When this happens, it begins to be possible to relive the past in such a way as to release the joyous energy denied in the inadequately negotiated separation crisis, and to make of gender no longer a fixing of us in the drama (with all the crippling consequences of gender-stereotyping that our society is at last beginning to question) but a function of the love between man and woman, which becomes in consequence a manifestation of the spirit in the flesh.

The whole of history could be seen as the complex struggle between the original habit binding people into its limited ways, whence come conflicts of every kind, and the gentle pressure of the spirit in people seeking to break out and free them. In that struggle, Christianity has thrown a definitive force onto the side of spirit, a force whose eruption was the raising of Jesus from the dead, which will be the theme of the fourth quadrant.

Of this human drama, the psyche has given us its own incomparable version in the form of myth. Myth is the way we used to talk about ourselves before we learned to lie. The myth that has dominated the Judaeo-Christian tradition whence our lives take their shape, is the story of the Fall in the Book of Genesis or Beginnings. What this myth above all reflects is the awesomeness of animal-life's becoming self-conscious. With this total change, the process of nature from conception to death ceases to be an instinctual, cosmically programmed affair, and becomes a *drama* in which the participants continually view each other and measure themselves by each other, in which nakedness begets shame, and the huge absorption of humankind with itself at the expense of its cosmic dimension has its beginning.

In becoming self-aware, in first learning to be 'I', I am drawn inexorably into a 'we' that I come to think of as the only world in which I am to assess myself. I am drawn into an exclusively human-defined reality. I am so drawn, because my individual existence is only half achieved and thus is forever looking to the mother whence it has only partially succeeded in separating itself. Thus dependent on the other for my sense of myself, I hardly suspect that there is a joy in being wholly myself, that there is a love for others in being wholly myself, of which the normal borrowed selfhood can give me no idea. That discovery, of self as luminous, is of the spirit. It is eventually to pervade the whole world and to wed us to the purpose of the universe. Of this triumph of spirit, the promise, as we shall see, is the crucifixion and resurrection of Jesus Christ.

75

22.

The structure of the Oedipal change

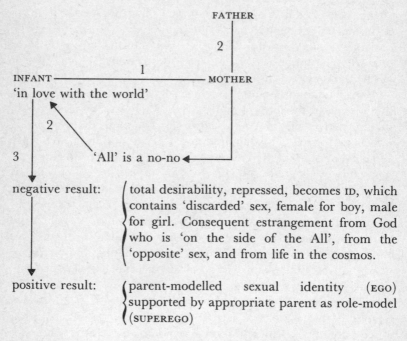

negative result: { total desirability, repressed, becomes ID, which contains 'discarded' sex, female for boy, male for girl. Consequent estrangement from God who is 'on the side of the All', from the 'opposite' sex, and from life in the cosmos.

positive result: { parent-modelled sexual identity (EGO) supported by appropriate parent as role-model (SUPEREGO)

Explanation
'In love with the world' is Margaret Mahler's description of the infant before the crisis. The Father–Mother love is in another dimension than the Infant–Mother love, represented by the vertical in contrast with the horizontal.

Explication
This represents the process in three stages. The 'negative result' is where we have to go, I think, to understand the meaning of original sin. But here a most important point has to be made. *The repression itself is not evil*: it is simply what is necessary at this stage of our

growth. We cannot grow to adulthood taking with us all the child's ebullience and love of life. 'You can't take it with you!' applies to growth as well as to death. Where evil, or sin, appears, is when my reduced desirability is taken to be *all that there is*, the whole thing, what life is all about. This generic sin, which permeates culture and society, is the denial of the whole-making Spirit of God (Holy Spirit) who sees me as one, not split into ego and id, and who is constantly at work in the world trying to make us one, in ourselves and with each other. Unity *within* the self creates unity *between* selves. This is especially clear (see the diagram) where the unity of man and woman is concerned, but it works right across the board. Just try to imagine a world in which men and women weren't in conflict – would anything in the world be untouched by this miracle?

This pressure for wholeness–oneness is the Holy Spirit (brilliantly, climatically manifest in the Christ event, as we shall see). The *counter-pressure*, sin, says, 'No, the Oedipal arrangement is absolute and final. Self-repression is what life is all about. There is no more. There is nothing else. Visions are moonshine. We are only half desirable, and half is OK.' Sin is the refusal to grow. It is the canonizing of the status quo. It outlaws *for ever* the child's sense of being all-desirable. Thus sin is not the *feeling* the child gets of not being all-desirable. It is the universal decision that this feeling is correct, is the thing to live by. Sin is self-denial. And this is the denial of God.

23.

The Fall

The most important thing about us humans, and therefore our deepest memory is that we are an animal species that became conscious. That has to have been a shattering experience.

The difference between an animal existence not aware of itself and a self-aware existence is so vast, so absolute, that it is difficult to think of any psychic continuity through the change, of any 'subject' *to* which the change happened. Yet a failure to stretch our minds at this point will mean that we shall never understand our human plight, potential and destiny.

The best method at this crucial point will be to ask what is the most striking thing about human growth. Freud's answer is not in doubt. He never ceased to be amazed that whereas animals come automatically to their maturity, humans do so dramatically. It is through a traumatic sociodrama that we develop into self-aware persons – the Oedipal crisis.

Let us see, then, what happens if we take this difference between automatic and dramatic growing, and think of these as occurring *successively*. Think of waking up doing deliberately what you were doing without any self-awareness. Think, in other words, of deliberate behaviour *as something new*, as experienced as something new. As something new and as something awful. The two go together. There is a sense that life, which yesterday was everywhere in everything, is now *in our hands*. There is a sense of enormous disproportion between the all-encompassing mystery enshrined in a 'forest of symbols' and its conduct 'in our hands'. A huge sense of failure is here, and a sense of the mystery as a total harmony now lost, fallen out of.

These are precisely the things highlighted in the story of the Fall. The immemorial rhythm of life in the garden is rudely interrupted by a drama: a command questioned, forbidden fruit found delightful and shared, eyes opened to the sexual novelty of shame, hiding from

78

the mystery now found menacing. The overall and overwhelming message is 'Life which pulses through the mysterious whole is in our hands to direct as we will, and how will we and how can we?' The myth of the Fall – in its many different cultural forms – expresses a reaction, far deeper than reason, to the anomaly of life's future being in our doubtful hands. We are feeling this anomaly anew in the nuclear age. But the anomaly is not new. It is the oldest, the original thing about us.

Just because the burden placed in our hands is altogether beyond us, we never get beyond *it* – and this is our 'original sin'. We prolong indefinitely the initial drama in which we came to self-awareness. We prolong indefinitely the Oedipal struggle with parents and past. We think permanently of ourselves in terms of the human drama, seeing ourselves in each others' eyes, blocking off the gracious insight into our unique reality as persons, the tremor of a happiness that vibrates through the universe.

Our consciousness clings stubbornly to its first focus, in the sociodrama, and resists the free forming of a new focus. The new focus forms under the gentle pressure of that directly felt awakening of our sense of being desirable, the sense of being desirable absolutely, because absolutely desired, of which I spoke in the second quadrant.

This great rhythm of the Fall is felt in the two crises of our infancy, the separation and the Oedipal crisis. For in recalling both these crises, we are awed by the phenomenon of 'conscious existence, consciousness of existence, depending for its quality on the participants in the drama'. In the first crisis, at age about one, the foundation is laid for how a person is to feel, till death, about existing separately, individually. How this feels, how good or not-so-good it feels, is dependent on the outcome of a dramatic dialogue between mother and infant at this stage, in which there will always be *some* communication of the mother's anxiety saying to the infant, 'Either be part of me or be on your own'. Thus no one emerges with a full sense of the goodness, the greatness, of being a conscious existence; and this diminished sense of goodness holds us in the dialogue whence it comes, so that we tend to look forever to the dialogue to complete itself, instead of attending to an inner voice making for true selfhood. Our life is at the mercy of the sociodrama, and deaf to the inner voice.

A couple of years later, the drama triangulates and complexifies. The infant's love for the mother, which emerges with the separation

79

crisis, finds itself puzzlingly challenged by another claim on the mother, the father's, that the child cannot understand. The child receives the message that the hedonism of being in love with mother is a 'no no', and thus the sense of being good and desirable, already diminished by an imperfect outcome of the separation crisis, is further diminished. This deficit is of course offset by the asset of newly acquired sexual identity and the capacity later to move in desire toward the opposite sex; but this movement will harbour an opposing tendency due precisely to the original wounding of our hedonism. The powerful desire for the other-sex – or for that matter the same-sex – partner needs to be balanced by an equally strong sense of the person's own desirability, whence alone true and creative desire proceeds; and this is lacking because of the early diminishment of our sense of being desirable.

Thus the generic diminishment of life due to life being 'in our hands' and concentrated in the human or first focus makes us resistant to the spirit of life that would lead us out into a far fuller existence, and to the hedonism which makes for the mutual surrender of man and woman. And these are not two resistances. The Christian tradition, in its molten scriptural origin, and the Christian mystical tradition, both discern a most intimate affinity of surrender to God with sexual surrender.

My purpose at this stage of the inquiry is to get as deep as possible a sense of generic or original sin, to get the feel and the shape of the human condition as one of less-than-full aliveness and of consequent concentration upon itself. By far the most dramatic way of presenting this condition is to see it in the trauma of the birth of self-awareness in the immemorially and inerrantly life-directed existence of the animal. From this trauma, we are still trying to recover. We find it difficult to listen to a God who is interested in so much more than recovery.

24.

What is sin?

Sin is saying no.
To what is sin saying no?
To the thing in me that wants to say yes.
What is it in me that wants to say yes?
It is my feeling of myself as being good.
Feeling myself as good, I want to go out to others.
This feeling of myself as good is the true feeling of myself.

As the great philosophy has always understood, to be is good,
'ens et bonum convertuntur', being and good are convertible terms.
'I am' means 'I am good'.

So that's where we've got so far: feeling myself as good, I want
to go out to others, to be good for others, and feeling myself as good
is feeling myself as truly I am.

So I'm not equally placed between a good self that wants to be
good and a bad self that doesn't. My good self is my true self, my
only self. So the only way not to want to go out to others is to go
against, to deny, to try to strangle, my feeling of myself as good.

This saying no to the feeling of myself as good is sin. Which is
where we came in.

Do you doubt this? Look at the Nazis and others who create hell
on earth for people. The dirty secret of the person who creates hell
for people is that deep down he loathes himself.

But this is only the beginning of the story. Or more accurately,
it's only the middle of the story. For we have to ask why we deny
our goodness to ourselves and thus to each other.

Traditionally, 'original sin' means the first denial, the first time
as it were. But previous to the first denial is the profound change in
feeling that invites the denial, the ambivalence of our sense of being
good, as we come to self-awareness in our animal nature.

And what is the cure for this enfeebled sense of our goodness?
Well, what makes being desirable is that it is the result of desire,

of the absolute desire that *by* desiring gives being to what it desires, that is, you and me.

So the cure for the human sickness and all its frightful conse-quences is *to experience myself as I am, as the desired of God.*

This experience is called grace, the felt presence of Creator to creature. It is God's creation happening in the person so that the person feels it. So it is called a new creation, the act of creation renewed. It is found in its fullness in Jesus, for he heard in himself the words, 'You are my beloved Son, in whom I have much pleasure.' So it is the Christ-self in us.

Into this Christ-self we are baptized. For its full flowering in us and in the world, we live in hope. This is *our* hope, the hope for ourselves – without which the thought of nuclear annihilation is not endurable. A spiritually mature person is one whom hope forbids to be overawed by this horror.

In brief: I want, above all else, the will of God; for I *am* the will of God. I seek the grace so to know myself.

25.

Rethinking original sin

The most radical experience we have of original sin is the memory of beginning to realize that desire could not be trusted. The *reason* desire cannot be trusted is that I am beginning to doubt my desirability. The sense of desirability, that directed me happily through life in infancy, now no longer works for me, for I am no longer just 'this body'. So my sense of being desirable ceases to be trustworthy as a guiding principle. I don't feel good with any conviction, and therefore I don't *do* what is good. So not feeling good is the *origin* of the *sin* of not doing what is good. It is the 'original sin', the origin of sin.

But how easy it is to *blame* the sense of being good and desirable that seems to have let us down. So we get the opposite version of what original sin is: original sin is the feeling of being good, it is 'pride', it is 'hedonism'. (With what great insight Mother Janet Erskine Stuart, the great educator in the Society of the Sacred Heart, said that she didn't think children should be taught humility.)

It is very easy to make this mistake. It is the easy way out to blame myself for 'coming on too strong', for over-believing in myself.

Because this mistake is so easily made, it has pervaded the Christian moral tradition, which has come to place original sin in feeling good instead of in feeling bad, which is where it should be placed, and the Christian moral tradition has laid itself open to those critics who accuse it of propagating the very disease it claims to be curing.

Thus we get the bad situation that while the best psychologists and counsellors are coming to understand the root of our evil as a bad self-image, Christians tend to say to them, 'You are leaving out original sin' – not realizing that these psychologists are, precisely, *pointing* to original sin. Mother Stuart got this one right. As of course have many other Christian teachers – at least in practice.

26.

Original sin – the doctrine and the voice

Moral evil, or sin, is enormously various and difficult to pin down. It has been said that the ways of evil are many, the way of truth one. Nevertheless it is possible, and necessary, to attempt to name the essence of sin, what sin fundamentally and always is.

To do this, we have to take a step back, behind and before sin, to see the situation in which sin arises and of which sin is the exploitation.

That situation is the reduced sense of my goodness that came with the Oedipal change, with the implanting, that is, of the seeds of adulthood in the child. *In* that situation, (a) I feel less than the child-sense of total desirability, (b) my innate zest for life is repressed and, from this repressed state, threatens my stability, (c) my vision of the opposite sex is warped through the repression of the other sex of myself, (d) *into* this process of adult-identity-through-rejection-of-child, there are inserted, as in fertile soil, all the biases and prejudices of my family, culture, race, nation, creed, etc. Sartre says that social class is inserted into the child's mind as an absolute.

Now in God's mind (a) one remains totally desirable because desired by God, (b) nothing in one, no feeling, no desire, is bad, (c) one and the other, woman and man are one, (d) we belong to the whole race of humankind, with no barriers between us. So God, the Holy (= whole-making) Spirit, is working to bring me to this true state of ourselves and of all humankind, through the multiple influences of prophets, poets, reformers of all kinds – in short, of all charismatic individuals who feel and know and try to show that the 'negative a b c d' is not *who we truly are* but is only *where we start* – that who we truly are, and where we are headed, is the 'positive a b c d' of God's vision.

Sin is the huge, universal, inertial force that resists this creative movement of the Spirit towards wholeness *in* people and oneness *among* people. How does this resistance work? It starts *in the mind*.

84

It starts as a mentality. In spite of a moralistic tendency in Christianity, for which the only sin is the sin we mean to do, Scripture is very clear that sin is a mentality which is too deeply ingrained for us to feel responsible for it – until we undergo what Scripture calls conversion.

And what is this sin-mentality? It comes very naturally. It consists in taking a, b, c, d, etc., and adding 'and that's the way it is'. (a) I *am not* very desirable, (b) my desire for ever-fuller life is an illusion, appropriately repressed, (c) conflict between the sexes is normal, and no radical change is to be expected here, (d) a person is a bundle of prejudices, and this is not radically open to change.

Sin, then, is a deep-seated reluctance to grow, to change, to open the mind, to respond to the promptings of the Holy Spirit. So it is a tendency to block the insight that would show me that I am painting myself into a corner needlessly. 'Needlessly?' I ask when the insight tries to get through. 'No, I've got to do it this way, it's always done this way, there is no other way.' That's the essential voice of sin. Bernard Lonergan speaks frequently of 'the flight from understanding'. That's closer to the real meaning of sin than any other description I know. We're afraid to understand, to see the way the world really is, because we'd have to change, and we are scared to change – and also very lazy. In fact Jung says that our dominant sin is indolence. This is the 'inertia' I spoke of above.

So subtle is this 'original sin' that it has managed to perform a brilliant trick or sleight-of-hand. It has persuaded religious people that the comment, 'And that's just the way it is,' is the voice of God. They say, 'You can't change human nature because of original sin.' That's absolutely true. But what it means is, 'Human nature is prevented from changing by original sin, *which is the belief that human nature cannot be changed.*'

What has happened is that the *voice* of original sin, 'That's just the way it is,' has masqueraded as the *doctrine* of original sin. With the disastrous consequence that preaching the doctrine of original sin is reinforcing the voice of original sin. Thus the preaching of the doctrine becomes iatrogenic – a 'therapy' that gives the patient the disease it purports to be curing.

This is no abstract speculation. It has dire practical consequences. Take the most urgent problem facing civilization today, the problem of nuclear war, of that final paroxysm of war that threatens all life as we know it. More and more people are coming

85

to see, as a character in one of Herman Wouk's books says at the end of World War II, 'Either we end war, or war will end us.' Thus they are trying to envisage that new idea, that utopian idea, a world without war. They are being vehemently opposed by a group of Catholics who regard themselves not only as orthodox but as one of the last bastions of Catholic orthodoxy. To aim for a world without war, say these Catholic stalwarts, is to deny the doctrine of original sin, because the doctrine of original sin implies that there will always be war. Wrong! *The voice* of original sin says, 'There will always be war,' just as in the past it said, 'There will always be slavery'. That's an original sinful statement, managing to masquerade as a church doctrine.

Finally here is a good example of a sinful situation, of the kind of corner we paint ourselves into under the subtle pressure of original sin – or original stupidity, the flight from understanding. It is the situation described by Harold Willens in his book, *The Trimtab Factor*, calling on the business community to end the nuclear arms race. He says that we are ruining our economy by drawing the Soviets into the one form of competition in which they can keep up with us.

27.

Getting rid of Limbo

The first and most important thing to be said about the doctrine of original sin is this. There would be no such doctrine of it were not for the experience of a totally new life, a new existence, a new creation, that the disciples of Jesus had and communicated to a growing community called the Church. The doctrine of original sin is a description of what life was like before, and without that new life. One of the great commentators on Paul's Letter to the Romans, Lagrange o.p., puts it well: It was only after they had been lifted up by Christ that people realized the abyss of wretchedness out of which they had been lifted. That abyss they saw as a state of self-exclusion from the Creator and consequent disharmony with each other and with the universe. They called it original sin. They saw it as something much more radical than the sins that people, or even peoples, commit. It was a cut-off-ness from God that was somehow woven into the human condition and had been so since the beginning of human time.

This is the doctrine of original sin. It is an integral part of Catholic and indeed all Christian belief. It is the doctrine of universal cut-off-ness from the source of our reality and well-being. When William Golding (author of *Lord of the Flies*) was awarded the Nobel prize, a leading critic said: 'I was flabbergasted – but on reflection, well yes, Golding's whole literary work has been to remind us of original sin, and this is appropriate to these dark times.'

This is the *doctrine* of original sin. It is symbolically expressed in the story of Adam and Eve, who are taken as *representative* of all humanity previous to the new Christ-formed humanity.

But once we state the doctrine, once we affirm the intuitive faith-insight that the human condition is this way, we must wonder *how it got to be this way*. A host of questions crop up: what went wrong, why, how? The handling of these questions pertains to *theology*: that is, not to *faith* but to the never-ending attempt to *explain* our faith to ourselves. There have been many such explanations of original sin, because its explanation has to use those tools for self-understanding and world-understanding that the culture of a given time provides, and there have been many different cultures between the time of Jesus and now.

None of these *explanations*, including of course the one I am offering, is *the doctrine itself*. They are a succession of theologies emanating from a succession of cultures. Theology is faith trying to explain itself. It explains itself differently in different epochs.

So how have believers tried to explain the deep sense that faith gives of the lack of God, the original sin, that faith begins to cure?

In the long period previous to our science-shaped culture, people were quite comfortable with the idea that the human race had started as a single adult pair planted by God in a garden. They were presumed to have had the kind of developed, civilized consciousness that we have. So the explanation, the theory, the theology, of how the great sin came to be in everyone, was that Adam and Eve committed the sin and it was passed down to all their descendants.

This explanation seemed the only one available, and so it became *in practice* the teaching of the Church. But theologians always recognized that there were flaws in the explanation, to say the least. For how could a state of sin be inherited? Jaroslav Pelikan, a leading Lutheran theologian, jocosely remarked that Augustine seemed to think of original sin as a kind of spiritual venereal disease. But the official teaching still was only an explanation. It was not the doctrine, the mysterious truth, of original sin.

The theory of evolution – for which the evidence is massive and continually growing – has done two things to the doctrine of original sin. It has made the old explanation nearly, but not quite, impossible to maintain. It is difficult to think of the human race starting in a state of perfection in a universe where nothing else does. But much more important, it has suggested a *new* explanation. The new explanation is that original sin is the universal, culturally propagated and reinforced, human response to the trauma of coming out of animality into self-awareness, into 'the knowledge of good and evil'. In this explanation, the profound unity of the whole human race – which we are coming more and more to appreciate – is emphasized. Each child re-enacts in him/herself the whole human drama.

Thus the new culture, the scientific culture, so profoundly different from its predecessors, enables us to reach a new *explanation* of the doctrine that the Church has held from its beginnings.

The most important practical consequence of the old explanation is that a newborn infant is in a state of sin and, if it dies unbaptized, cannot be saved. This is a monstrous idea. When I was editing *The Downside Review*, a leading English theological journal, I published a book-length article by a Dutch theologian showing that this idea of 'Limbo' never really made it into the mainstream of Catholic tradition. The so-called doctrine has disappeared – into limbo. It never really was a doctrine. It was the logical consequence of an *explanation* of a doctrine.

But as in economics, bad money drives out good. If you mention original sin, people think not of *Lord of the Flies* or of the enormous tragic perversity of history, but of babies and Limbo. Perhaps the main task of theology is to make our faith become adult.

28.

The unorthodoxy of fundamentalism

The religious purpose of the story of the Fall is to provide the deepest diagnosis of our human plight, to set this plight in the divine perspective, to say 'what's wrong with the world' from the point of view of our true nature as God-originated, God-directed, and God-destined beings.

Now a thing we are coming to understand today is, that the origin of destructive attitudes and actions in a person is very deep. This source of evil is a resistance to growth, a reluctance to change, a refusal to live more adequately. Freud discovered in his patients a strong resistance to getting well. Everyone wants to *feel* well, but paradoxically often opposes that opening-up of new possibilities which *leads* to getting well.

Now this resistance is a 'not wanting to understand', and this is a very odd kind of 'not wanting'. Normally we are only aware of wanting or not wanting something when we have already understood what it is we want or don't want. But what we are concerned with here is a fundamental resistance to change and to new life, that *prevents* understanding.

Now it seems pretty clear that it is this fundamental resistance to change and growth that is 'what's wrong with the world', that lies at the base of racial and class and religious hatreds, to say nothing of marital and sexual tangles. Clearly this diagnosis of human evil is much more radical, that is, nearer to the roots, than one which only looks at bad attitudes and actions that are quite deliberate and *presuppose* understanding I mean, the refusal that *precedes* and *prevents* understanding is more radical than the refusal that *presupposes* understanding.

But if the religious diagnosis of our plight is supposed to be the most radical, it must address itself to this deeper level that we are talking about, where resistance precedes and precludes understanding. It cannot confine itself to straight deliberate sin, which is only the tip of the iceberg of human evil.

Now a literal interpretation of the story of the Fall does precisely this. It says that all that goes wrong in the world is because of, has its roots in, a definite, deliberate decision taken by our first parents. In other words, it fails to go any deeper, in the search for the source of evil, than the deliberate choice against good. Thus a literal interpretation of the story is precisely not a radical diagnosis of our plight.

But the doctrine of original sin, if it expresses a vision of sin in the ultimate perspective of God, *is* a radical diagnosis of our plight.

Therefore a literal interpretation of the story of the Fall is incompatible with the doctrine of original sin. It treats superficially what that doctrine treats at the greatest depth.

This cannot be the only instance where a literal interpretation of the Bible contradicts the Christian faith – that faith which nourishes itself on the Bible as myth, as the place of healing symbols, as the poetry of God.

29.

The arms race, game theory, and original sin*

The most serious problem facing the world today, and at any time in its history, is the galloping arms race between the two superpowers. There is wide agreement about this.

But while most people agree on the seriousness of the problem and on the mounting danger of nuclear calamity, the tendency is to go on to say something like this: Clearly there need to be arms negotiations. But how can these proceed, since neither of the superpowers trusts the other?

It is necessary, however, to examine the notion of *what trust is* that underlies the above statement. There are sound reasons for saying that it is seriously defective, that trust between nations, and between political groups generally, is not the *kind* of thing that the maker of the statement clearly has in mind. Not surprisingly, the kind of trust she/he has in mind is the only kind of trust we deal with in our ordinary personal relations, namely a willingness to put oneself at risk, a becoming-vulnerable to the other. The essence of this kind of trust is that it goes beyond one's rationally perceived self-interest. And the assumption made by people when they say the superpowers cannot trust one another is that the above generous attitude is sadly lacking in the tough world of international relations. But there are sound reasons for saying that there is a kind of trust that does *not* conflict, as the generous trusting of a spouse in a critical situation, with rationally perceived self-interest, does *not* put the trusting one at risk and make him vulnerable to total betrayal.

The 'sound reasons' arise from what is called game theory, an

* For the substance of this chapter I depend on 'Trust: Missing Link in the Politics of Peace' by Michael McNulty, SJ, a very important essay published in *The Woodstock Report* No. 4, March 1984. The quotes are from this essay.

92

approach to problem solving that is rapidly gaining in sophistication and momentum at this time. Let us start with an example:

Suppose that a revolutionary group and an arms supplier are to complete a transaction, and that for security reasons they cannot meet face to face. The plan is that the revolutionaries are to leave a certain sum of money at a certain location and the arms dealer is to leave the appropriate supply of weapons at another location, sufficiently separated from the first that neither can verify the other's action at the time the arms or money are to be left. Clearly each has two choices, to keep the bargain or to double-cross the other. If the revolutionaries pay the money, it is clearly in the interest of the arms dealer not to deliver the arms, since then the dealer will have both the money and the arms. And the situation is clearly symmetrical for the revolutionaries. If they commit the double-cross, *they* will have the arms and the money. But if it is in both their interests to double-cross the other, the transaction will never take place, and neither will receive any benefit at all.

This parable describes a formal situation called a prisoner's dilemma in the branch of applied mathematics called game theory. The point about this class of games is that if *all* the players do the untrusting thing, they all lose. Thus mistrust does not coincide with rationally perceived self-interest. If everyone stays on the safe side, all lose out: the revolutionary group gets no arms, the supplier no cash.

Now the case for trust as the efficient way to act is greatly strengthened when the rebels and the suppliers need regular supplies of arms and cash respectively, so that future transactions are foreseen. And of course arms negotiations between the superpowers are of this repetitive kind, not a one-shot deal. We should therefore attend especially to what we may learn from game theory in this area of repeated deals, where mutual trust is more clearly profitable to both sides than in the one-shot deal.

But how is such mutual trust to be promoted? Robert Axelrod of the University of Michigan has done extensive research on this question by means of computer simulation of repeated prisoners' dilemma strategies (his research is discussed in *The Evolution of Cooperation*, published by Basic Books). Surprisingly, the long-run champion was a strategy called TIT FOR TAT (submitted for Axelrod's study by Anatol Rapoport, and encoded in a simple, four-line BASIC program). TIT FOR TAT begins by cooperating, i.e. by trusting its partner on the first round. On each succeeding round, it does what its partner did on the previous round. That's all there is to it; yet TIT FOR TAT was clearly more effective in the long run than a great many other more complicated strategies. Axelrod discovered that a number of effective strategies had several characteristics in common: they were 'nice', that is, they *began* by trusting their partner; they were 'vindictive', that is, they punished defection; and they were 'forgiving', that is, they went back to being nice after they had inflicted punishment. (Interestingly enough, a strategy for reducing cold-war tensions called GRIT, Graduated Reciprocation in Tension Reduction, proposed by Charles E. Osgood in 1962, has all these characteristics. It bears a remarkable resemblance to the philosophy of détente that characterized American foreign policy in the early 1970s.)

What conclusion should be draw from this? It seems from these results that far from being irrational, mutual trust is the *only* way of establishing cooperation for mutual benefit. But there is more: an essential element in establishing trust is some kind of unilateral initiative without preconditions. This means that the establishment of mutual trust begins with unilateral trust, and we need to make clear here that we are not talking about gambling. Gambling weighs the odds; trust always involves the possibility of losing more if you are betrayed than you would gain if your trust is rewarded. Anwar Sadat's courageous gesture in travelling to Israel in 1977 resulted in the return of the Sinai and the normalization of relations between Egypt and Israel, yet Sadat as much as anyone must have been aware of the potential for disaster contained in his deed.

Studies carried out by Morton Deutsch in the early 1960s on the relationships between trust and personality suggest that trust and trustworthiness tend to go together, whereas those who are reluctant to trust tend also to be untrustworthy, authoritarian, cynical, prejudiced, and exploitative. (An illustration of my principle, that people who are unhappy with others are unhappy with themselves.) These results suggest that reluctance to trust is related to a number of other traits that are destructive of political cohesion and therefore of cooperative behaviour for common ends. It is not a great leap from here to the conclusion that trust is pre-eminently rational in the sphere of political activity.

Can the kind of trust I have spoken of here be absolutely

justified? Clearly not. But the alternative is at best continued non-cooperation in a variety of social spheres in which cooperation may well be essential for survival. It might be well to recall the words of Dorothee Soelle (in *Cross Currents*, Summer 1983): 'The truth is that one side must begin, one of us must drop the threats, one of us must take a tiny step forward, *alone*. Those who think bilaterally are condemned to impotence; they will never break the circle. Who is in a position to take the step forward, unilaterally, *toward* peace?'

The foregoing is by no means unrelated to the concept of original sin that we are unfolding. Once you finalize, and declare the unalterable *reality*, the *tendency* to mutual suspicion implicit in the 'negative a b c d', then a realistic approach to human relations will not have much room for trust. Especially will this be the case for relations between nations. And the worst case of all would seem to be the huge world powers, the USA and the USSR. Yet there exists, on the basis of game theory, a strong case for saying that a measure of trust between the superpowers is not only possible but necessary for the security of each. If this is true, if McNulty's argument is sound, then the 'realism' that normalizes mistrust is a false realism. And of course it is! For it is the 'realism' of original sin. It is the realism you get when original sin, the flight from understanding, is allowed full sway. It is a 'realism' that would bury civilization in radioactive rubble. I've heard it called 'crackpot realism'. It has a fatal appeal for a certain type of politician.

Jacques Maritain was pointing to this pernicious pseudo-realism when he said that the worst thing we have inherited from Machiavelli is the notion – very prevalent today – that morality, trust, decent behaviour, is for idealists and does not belong in the market place and in politics. Anyone who believes this is listening to the voice of original sin, the original lie about the human condition, the lie that absolutizes the multiple bias to which that condition is indeed prone owing to the dramatic, traumatic, risk-laden manner of our coming to self-awareness.

In short –

False: Original sin *makes* trust between nations impossible and wars inevitable.

True: Original sin *says* trust between nations is impossible and wars are inevitable.

The voice of original sin is original sin itself whispering in our ear. The doctrine of original sin is the warning about this voice in us. Obviously they are not the same, yet they are constantly confused. It's like saying that the warning of an epidemic is the epidemic.

Incidentally, it always amazes me that the Christians for whom the *doctrine* of original sin means that human nature is unalterable (which is what *the voice* is saying) also manage to believe – presumably in some other and unrelated part of their brain – that human nature *has* been changed radically, by Jesus Christ.

30.

Flesh and spirit according to Paul

My point is that you should live in accord with the spirit and you will not yield to the cravings of the flesh. The flesh lusts against the spirit and the spirit against the flesh; the two are directly opposed. This is why you do not do what your will intends. If you are guided by the spirit, you are not under the law. It is obvious what proceeds from the flesh: lewd conduct, impurity, licentiousness, idolatry, sorcery, hostilities, bickering, jealousy, outburts of rage, selfish rivalries, dissensions, factions, envy, drunkenness, orgies, and the like. I warn you, as I have warned you before: those who do such things will not inherit the kingdom of God. In contrast, the fruit of the spirit is love, joy, peace, patient endurance, kindness, generosity, faith, mildness, and chastity. Against such there is no law! Those who belong to Christ Jesus have crucified their flesh with its passions and desires. Since we live by the spirit, let us follow the spirit's lead. Let us never be boastful, or challenging, or jealous toward one another. (Galatians 5:16ff.)

Most people on hearing this famous passage read in church, probably interpret it in the following manner: 'There is a spiritual part of me that inclines to unselfish behaviour and worship, and delights in spiritual things; and there is another part of me that is centred on physical gratification in all its forms; and these two are opposed, engaged in a tug-of-war for my consent. The purpose of prayer and spiritual discipline is to ensure the victory of the first, higher part of me, over the second, lower part.'

The difficulty with this interpretation, that has been the prevalent one in Christian history, is that it implies that physical gratification, fleshly pleasure which God has invented, is opposed to God. It puts God at enmity with half of his own creation.

Fortunately, however, it is clear on strictly scholarly grounds that this interpretation badly misses Paul's meaning.

'The flesh', for Paul, is not 'a part of my nature' but 'a partial view of my whole nature'. It is a way of thinking, and acting accordingly. It is a whole philosophy of life. And the main point is that this philosophy of life excludes, ignores, has no time or place for, a larger view of life to which I am being drawn by the spirit.

But one can't simply equate 'the flesh' with 'a narrow view and way of life'. If words mean anything, the flesh is *to do with* sex and other physical pleasures. And this raises the crucial question: What is the connection between 'a narrow view and way of life' and the pleasures of the flesh? That's obvious, someone might say. The pleasures of the flesh, *regarded as what life is all about*, make for a narrow view and way of life.

Now this is getting somewhere – it makes the point that will prove crucial, that sin consists in treating a partial view of life as the whole. But what does it mean, *positively*, to embrace the pleasures of the flesh *within a larger view and way of life*. The explanation so far offered (by the 'someone' of the last parargraph) has had little to say about this. We are still waiting to have the *belief*, that pleasure is God-invented and good, spelt out in a coherent ethic of sexual and other pleasure. Our Christian ethics have made a dismal showing at translating *into ethics* the statement in Genesis, 'God saw all that he had made, and it was very good'. What is the sex-life of a saint like? On the Aristotelian principle that the only way to get a real idea of justice is to watch a just person in action, this question means, 'What is the Christian way of sex? What is the Christian way with all the other pleasures of life?'

Now this question implies that pleasure, in all its forms, *has a wider context* in which it could and sometimes does happen, in which it would be the creature's response to a pleasure-creating God. Have you ever experienced, or thought you experienced, sexual pleasure in this way? Would you say that this was widespread? A clear look at the sexual scene – at least at its more conspicuous – and the power-scene and the money-making scene, would seem to warrant the conclusion that *there is a narrower context* in which these activities 'normally' take place, a context that is widely prevalent. What is this narrower context? This is the crux of the matter.

The narrower context is 'the set of attitudes into which the child, crossing the Oedipal frontier, begins rapidly to grow'.

This context, this cluster of attitudes, is not sinful. It is the unavoidable first shaping of our adult life. But it is not the final, God-intended shape. There is in us a powerful tendency to *regard* it as the final shape, as the human reality *simpliciter*. The consent to this tendency *is* sin – social, individual, social and individual inextricably intertwined. Sin is the refusal to grow, to take *new* shapes.

Sin, then, means acting out the 'attitudes' – of self-negation (a), of repression (b), of sexual estrangement (c), of cultural-social-familial biases (d) ('negative a b c d') – *as though they defined the total moral universe*. Behind the insatiable lust of the promiscuous and the power-hungry and the money-greedy, is the voice that asks, inaudibly, and with concealed desperation, 'What else is there?' *That* is the voice of original sin. Living by the dictates of that voice is what Paul means by 'living according to the flesh'.

The reason why some of the more spectacular sinners have had spectacular conversions is that the question 'What else is there?', activated by a colourful moral life, sometimes makes itself heard and is surprised by an answer from an unexpected quarter.

It follows from all this that all sin is spiritual, to do with the spirit. There is no such thing, in strict theory, as 'sexual sin'. The sin in what is *called* sexual sin is the sin of self-closure to spiritual growth, the self-closure that lies imperceptibly behind 'sexual sin'. Conversely the action of 'the Spirit', of divine inspiration, is not directly upon our sexual and other passions but upon the set of attitudes that we think of as the unchanging parameters of those passions. Thus there is not a tug-of-war between a 'higher' and a 'lower' part of us. There is a tension between our radical desire to grow and our inertial tendency to stay as we are.

Our radical desire to grow, under the pressure of God's Spirit, is what Paul means by 'the spirit'. Our inertial tendency to stay as we are is what Paul means by 'the flesh'. The only problem is that Paul, like many geniuses, like all first-formulators of a dynamic new idea, does not make clarifying distinctions. What I am suggesting he means by 'living by the flesh' in the above passage is 'living by our appetites,– which are God-invented and good, within a context of attitudes, which are necessary to the first shaping of ourselves and therefore good *as* a beginning – as though these attitudes were final and constituted the total human moral universe.'

I seriously suggest that our modern psychological self-knowledge does provide us with just the category that is needed to explicate Paul's passionate rhetoric of flesh and spirit. That category is 'the

Oedipally initiated but not final shaping of our attitudes to ourselves, to each other, and to life'.

The importance of the fact that we are essentially *beings in time*, growing beings, cannot be asserted too strongly. It is absolutely central to all I have written above. And it is an insight special to our time. In the ancient world we thought of ourselves in space. Only later have we come really to think of ourselves in time. If I am essentially a grower, my refusal to grow is a denial of my nature: this is sin.

Original sin, 'living by the flesh', is a stuckness of humankind at its first stage of consciousness, a kind of universal arrested development. It is called sin quite appropriately, because for an essentially growing being to refuse to grow is to go against its nature, and that is precisely what sin is.

And since by sin I am *confining myself* to this 'half-life', I am *compelled* to live out its biases by getting the better of others, etc. Thus for Paul – and for our modern understanding of life under repression – there is a compulsive quality in life 'according to the flesh'. What he is always saying to his converts is, 'You don't have to live this way any more. You are free;' Thus he does not say, 'Live by the spirit. *Don't* follow the lusts of the flesh' (which, by the way, covers all the seven capital sins). He says, 'Live by the spirit, *and then you won't* find yourselves following the lusts of the flesh.' And when he invites them to look back on their pre-converted lives, he's not saying, 'Look what wicked people you were!' but, 'Remember that wretched trap you were in? How else could you have behaved, closed in the way you were?'

When you recall, with horror, something very low and mean you once did, try saying to yourself, 'How else could I have behaved, seeing how shut-in I then was?' That stimulates the desire to get freer still, instead of concentrating you morbidly on the past.

Finally, the compulsive nature of our half-life gives us the key to one of the most fascinating things in Paul: the way he talks about 'the Law'. For Paul, even the holy law of God is powerless to cure us. All it can do is observe the things that sin compels us to do, and try to compel us not to do them! And, as he observes at one point, the counter-compulsion sometimes reinforces the compulsion (Romans 7:7–11). He finds a parallelism between the law of God and the 'law of sin'. Psychologically they both operate at the same level, where no cure of our condition is possible.

What it really comes down to is this.

1. There is the incomparably fuller life open to us – life 'in the spirit'.

2. There is the lesser life *than which* this life in the spirit is incomparably fuller.

3. This lesser life cannot itself be wrong or evil or sinful.

4. Sin consists in confining ourselves to this smaller life, blocking our sense of the spirit. This is living *by* the flesh – as opposed to living *in* the flesh.

5. Thus confined, we have to get satisfaction through the 'negative a b c d' – that is, through denying the fuller good in us (a), repressing our feeling (b), winning the sexual conflict (c), prevailing over others in the whole area of our biases (d).

6. Hence 'living by the flesh' is compulsive, and the countercompulsion of the law is powerless to save us, and can make things worse.

Why not go back now and reread that passage of Paul. It is one of the classics of the Christian life. By learning to read it with the above structure in the back of our mind, we could salvage it from centuries of Christian misunderstanding.

31.

The first and second focus of consciousness

We start our conscious life very powerfully focused on each other in the human drama. (A new book, shortly to appear, by Lowell Edmunds of Johns Hopkins University, gives versions of the Oedipal myth from all over the world, obviously not dependent on the Greek source.) So strong is this first focus, that it is with difficulty that we shift to a new focus, notwithstanding the fact that this new focus is of our most primitive sense of ourselves as, amazingly and wonderfully, alive. We start heavily inclined to measure ourselves by each other, and this builds up a centredness on the human drama that ignores the primitive fact of our existence in the cosmos.

Here is how one poet has grasped this idea. In 'The Tower beyond Tragedy', Robinson Jeffers, a badly neglected modern American poet, gives his own version of the Oresteia. At the end, Electra and Orestes face each other at dawn by the hillside. Together they have done the ultimate forbidden deed – killed the Mother. Electra says:

> . . . We two of all the world, we alone,
> Are fit for each other, we have so wrought . . .

This total breach with the past is a bond between them that they must seal with an incestuous royal marriage, and declare a new era for the House of Mycenae. There is a moment of passion, but then Orestes says:

> Here is the last labor
> To spend on humanity. I saw a vision of us move in the dark:
> all that we did and dreamed of
> Regarded each other, the man pursued the woman, the woman
> clung to the man, warriors and kings

Strained at each other in the darkness, all loved or fought inward,
    each one of the lost people
Sought the eyes of another that another should praise him; sought
    never his own but another's; the net of desire
Has every nerve drawn to the center, so that they writhed like a
    full draught of fishes, all matted
In the one mesh; when they look backward they see only a man
    standing at the beginning.
Or forward, a man at the end; or if upward, men in the shining
    bitter sky striding and feasting,
Whom you call Gods . . .
It is all turned inward, all your desires incestuous, the woman
    the serpent, the man the rose-red cavern,
Both human, worship forever . . .

ELECTRA   You have dreamed wretchedly.

ORESTES   I have seen the dreams of the people and not dreamed
    them.
As for me, I have slain my mother.

The last lines of the play have haunted me for some time:

She turned and entered the ancient house. Orestes walked in the
    clear dawn; men say that a serpent
Killed him in high Arcadia. But young or old, few years or many,
    signified less than nothing
To him who had climbed the tower beyond time, consciously,
    and cast humanity, entered the earlier fountain.

32.

The conundrum of the flesh

So what *does* Paul mean by the flesh? Clearly he is referring to physical pleasures, satisfaction of sensual craving, craving for power, etc. – among other things.

But Paul says, 'In the flesh we cannot please God' (Rom. 8:8).

So what we seem to have is the proposition that sensual pleasure is not pleasing to God – who created sensual pleasure!

Clearly we have a problem here.

At this point, along comes that deadly enemy, that promoter of the flight from understanding, the Jovial Simplifier, who says, 'It's simply that we mustn't *live* for pleasure.' It's quite true that we shouldn't live for pleasure, that such a life is largely wasted. But this statement of the Jovial Simplifier misses the real question, which is: What role *should* pleasure play in our lives? And why, when it is playing this role, is it no longer 'of the flesh' even though it is still, clearly fleshly pleasure?

What Paul means by 'the flesh' and 'the deeds of the flesh' is the whole gamut of desire and pursuit and satisfaction *taking place within a situation of confinement*, of arrest at the first, Oedipal, people-with-people-mutually-defining stage of consciousness. In *that* world it is impossible to please God, because in that world a person has not yet discovered him/herself and is still at the beginning of the journey that ends in God.

It is because of this heavy confinement that our desires put us in competition and ceaseless conflict. We are shut in, psychologically on top of each other. Our desires are limitless and need the limitless breathing-space of the spirit. Closed in, they make us mutually destructive. In the nuclear crisis, we see this drama on a global scale. We have carried the exclusive concentration on our inter-human drama to a point where our wretched wars can plunge the planet into a 'nuclear winter'.

What went wrong after Paul was that people forgot *why* Paul said that our pursuit of satisfaction was mutually divisive. They forgot *what* he saw wrong in the human tangle of lust, power, money, etc. They forgot the second stage, of life in the spirit, *through stopping short of which* the human scene is so full of conflict, tragedy and misery. They forgot the mystical. The dropping-out of the mystical dimension is the greatest disaster in the Christian ethical tradition. It compels us to distort Paul's meaning, for if we don't see the high confining wall that he sees making us mutually destructive in pursuit of our desires, we are bound to see the destructiveness *in the desires themselves*. This is why the Christian ethic has never succeeded in wholly and unequivocally affirming the goodness of sexual pleasure. The absence of the mystical sense, and the absence of a Christian hedonism, are the two sides of the same coin.

And when we turn to Aristotle, we find that pleasure, far from being grudgingly accepted or regarded as of secondary importance, is the indispensable sign that something is being done properly. If you don't enjoy doing something, you haven't yet learned how to do it. Pleasure is the perfection of an act. It follows that the more skills and virtues a person possesses, the greater that person's capacity for pleasure.

This profound insight of Aristotle has enjoyed scant recognition in the Christian ethical tradition. Indeed, we have come to think the opposite – that the sign of an act being virtuous is that it's difficult and painful. In fact, this is the sign that one is only a beginner. Leo Buscaglia doesn't seem to find it difficult to hug strangers.

33.

Two pictures of self

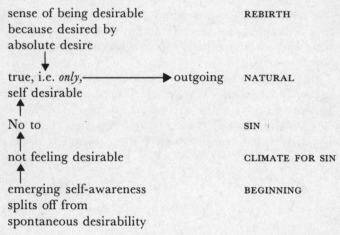

FALSE

good self ──────────▶ outgoing

bad self

TRUE

sense of being desirable   REBIRTH
because desired by
absolute desire
        ↓
true, i.e. *only*, ──────────▶ outgoing   NATURAL
self desirable
        ↑
No to   SIN
        ↑
not feeling desirable   CLIMATE FOR SIN
        ↑
emerging self-awareness   BEGINNING
splits off from
spontaneous desirability

The downward arrow shows the process of divine therapy for our sick condition, which we are going to be looking at next (and last). Briefly, only the *experience* of being created, of being desirable because desired, can cure us radically. For this experience reconnects self-awareness with the whole cosmic order out of which we have come into temporarily separate existence. It cures sin *at its root*, which is pre-sin ('BEGINNING').

It must require a vast simplicity
to live through all the moods of self and time
with one by whose desire one is desirable.

The question 'Where does God come in?' is, I suggest, an unhelpful question. What I mean by saying this is suggested by an observation I make in connection with Centring Prayer, when people complain that this is simply Transcendental Meditation with belief added. Centring Prayer is not TM with belief added. TM is Centring Prayer with belief subtracted. Involvement with total ultimate mystery is the primary datum of consciousness, as Voegelin insists and as our culture strenuously tries to deny.

34.

Re-living approaches rebirth

What is meant by the stabbing recall of the past that I have with growing frequency? In these moments, I do not so much remember as relive. In remembering, the past *situation*, the scene, is recalled, but how *I* was in the scene is not recalled. In fact, the past 'I' is now being judged as though she/he were someone else, as though she/he were a character in that play whom I am now censuring for acting so foolishly. But in the reliving experience, I *am* that character, now. I, with my present sense of myself as responsible, am that character who is doing the long-past action, which I now regard not as foolish but as myself trying to get free, now. There is in fact a paradox here. The more I feel inclined to say 'How foolish!', the less there is anyone there to have *been* foolish; whereas the more I am now living that character and doing that foolish action now responsibly, the less relevant it seems to say 'How foolish!' The more responsible I feel for that behaviour, the less judgmental I feel about it, whether to call it right or wrong.

It is, in fact, as though I were choosing all of my life, even from its beginning. It is as though the consciousness that, unnoticed, unifies each moment, were beginning to insist upon *its own* continuing identity throughout the successive moments. *I* cannot be a succession of moments. To the extent that my life appears in retrospect as a succession, I am not myself. How often must consciousness perform, over and over again, its funcion of unifying *each situation*, before I realize what it is, who I am? The moment of realization is when consciousness, that already and in everybody creates 'reality' for me, comes into its own.

The Hindu myth, according to which the soul chooses the womb to take flesh in, seems to us absurd. And yet the process of awakening-to-itself that I am here attempting to describe seems to be extending my present sense of responsibility backward. At the extremity of the process I would now be choosing the womb I was carried in. The researches of Frank Lake in this area are relevant. Twenty years ago, he was using LSD to solicit from patients a memory of the womb.

Might we not extend this process of self-discovery to the whole race? Consciousness, as it first comes to be in the hominid, could be regarded as having a 'simple' existence, before it broke down into the double role of unifying the world and being itself at the same time, before it was forced to forget itself in the process of unifying the surroundings, turning the animal's environment into the human's world. Then begins the long, seemingly endless road of differentiation, of organizing the masses of data in the different ways appropriate to different levels of culture. During all this period, consciousness is the unacknowledged, ever-active servant, on whose continuous labours all our creeds and worldviews and meaningful projects depend. Finally, consciousness is to become itself.

In so doing, it realizes its beginning. Consciousness, in the laboured process of differentiating and organizing, harks *back* to a fullness of itself as it looks *forward* to a fullness of itself. The myth of the Garden, of the Golden Age, expresses this backward yearning of consciousness. Justus George Lawler finds this rhythm, from the full, through the diverse, to the full, in all poetic cadence (cf. *Celestial Pantomime*).

The most potent source of confusion at the present time is that some people are feeling a stirring of the final stage, of consciousness becoming itself, while others are not. The confusion is maximal when both parties to the human debate are religious believers. For the religious mystic, the absoluteness, transcendence and infinity of God affirms itself in his/her prayer experience. He/she knows transcendence in a way that is not known by one who has so far learned from consciousness only to differentiate. For the latter, the transcendence of God is affirmed only by saying that God is separate from the world. For him/her, God is prayed to. But for the mystic, God is prayed by, God prays him/her. Indeed, God's praying of me is the meaning of 'the consciousness of consciousness'. Contemplating, says St John of the Cross, is receiving. And of what can consciousness-become-itself receive but of the mystery whereby it is? But a person talking out of this new self-awareness will be heard by one who is not 'there' as not stating the transcendence of God in the only way in which he/she *can* state it, namely the way of setting God over-against the self and its world.

The Fourth Quadrant

35.

Focusing for the fourth quadrant

What is the universal human captivity, which theology calls the condition of original sin?

To answer this question, we must perform a rather intrepid feat of memory. My earliest recollection is of people very close to me – mother, father, family. And my earliest *self*-recollection is of looking at myself through their eyes, modelling myself on them, measuring myself by them, learning from them who I was. This seeing of myself in, and as part of, the human drama, is the first focus of our consciousness.

Being our first focus, this way of seeing ourselves is enormously powerful. So it has a strong tendency to perpetuate itself right on into our adult life. Society and culture reinforce this tendency. For not only do children see themselves in relation to adults, but adults see themselves as 'over' children. So society and culture encourage us to measure ourselves off each other, to refer ourselves to the ongoing human drama, to regard the world we make together as *the* world. A visitor from another world, watching our behaviour and reading our books and newspapers, might exclaim, 'My God, these humans seem to think of nothing but themselves, nothing but the endless thing that's going on between them! Can't they see the stars?'

And, if you think about it, it becomes clear that this view-of-myself-through-others can only be a beginning. For I am I. I am unique. I am not defined by my parents, my family, my nation, my class, my creed, my profession. I am a destiny beyond all these things. So to grow, to 'put away the things of a child', is to become myself, unique, having mystery alone for my source, spirit alone for my life.

This next great step, this second focus, this entry into our true, free self, we resist. We cling to the 'first focus' as the first thing we know and the only thing we know. There is a deep reluctance to

113

grow to our true and terrifying stature. This reluctance, spread across the whole of humankind, and having roots beyond our reach, is the state of original sin. Sin is our deep-seated refusal to grow.

In its original form, sin is a diminished sense of our greatness, a radical mistrust of life which resists change and growth (the essential marks of life), blocks new and liberating insights, keeps us captive within our first, Oedipal, each-other-regarding parameters, and thus perpetuates vicious – that is cyclic – routines and pursues selfish courses even to our own detriment. Indeed original sin is our deathwish, our flight from the understanding through which life could come to us. We distinguish – and have to – between 'sins' and 'mistakes'. But original sin is at that deepest level where this distinction has not yet arisen: it is an original resistance that is, indistinguishably, stupid and malicious.

When you read about the insane folly of the nuclear arms race and a world already burned up by hunger, and when you realize that the list is endless and includes your own unaccountable behaviour, you are reading about humanity's state of arrested development.

The staggering assertion of the Gospel of Jesus Christ is that even this condition is curable, and that the cure exists, in a people who remember one who stretched our life beyond the limits we set upon it and, beyond those limits, 'revealed the resurrection'.

36.

Introducing the fourth quadrant

From the foregoing it may appear that the consciousness that we have now, what might be called Adamic consciousness, is only the beginning of consciousness. The you that is now is only the beginning of you. If I try to describe myself, I find myself saying what I am not. I am not my body. I am not other people. I am not the world. I am not the universe.

What then am I? What *is* this reality that I call 'I'? I cannot say. And the reason I cannot say lies in all those things I have had to separate myself from in order to begin to be myself. For the separate self is only half a self. The other half is my body, is the others, is the world, is the universe.

To be rejoined with that other half is the state that is sometimes called cosmic consciousness. People who have had an inkling of this condition speak of an abrupt ending of the sense of self as isolated, as a citadel, as an enclosure; instead, the person feels identified with the whole pulsating energy of the cosmos. And this is not a *loss* of identity, but a *finding* of identity hitherto lost in isolation. For how can I be said to lose identity when *I* feel identical with all there is.

When Jesus said we must lose ourselves in order to find ourselves, what he is saying we have to lose is the self we have come to think of as separated from the whole because it had to *start* separate from the whole. I mean, just because we *start* being selves by separation, we assume that that is how we are to *stay* being ourselves. And it is not. The self is a destiny whose completion is cosmic. Do you really think that sunset over the mountains that filled you with peace was meant to be only a *view*? No, it was a premonition of your true home, which is the whole universe.

In that home, I am one with my body, with all humankind, with all the universe. And thus identified, I experience the hunger of being for the inventor of being. Consciousness, spilling over its temporary citadel into all the universe, stretches ecstatically toward absolute consciousness in which the universe is grounded.

So instead of thinking, as the catechism made us think, of the soul as all wound up with the body in this life and getting at last free of the body at death, we should think almost the exact opposite. In this life, we are separated from our bodiliness. In death, we are reunited with our bodiliness and with the whole universe of which it is a part.

This too is how we should think of beloved relatives and friends who have died. How did that ridiculous notion grow up of the heavenly condition symbolized by sitting on a damp cloud playing a harp? The answer is clear. Unable to think beyond the present, temporal and temporarily separated self, we mentally plonk it down 'on the other side' and find it something to do.

We need to think cosmic consciousness, as our destiny and as the life into which our loved ones are being drawn. And consciousness is not what we know: it is *how* we know. A distorted consciousness knows badly. A free consciousness knows well. It takes *cosmic* consciousness to know God, to experience in its full force the love that God is. Cosmic consciousness is the liberating of desire for the perfection of consciousness. And so our final question in this book is: How, through Christ, do we enter cosmic consciousness? To this question we now proceed.

37.

How the new life was born

We have defined the human plight, original sin, as a condition of arrested development. We now proceed to show that the story of Jesus, which is the story of our salvation or liberation from this plight, is to be understood as the release of this arrested development.

We have seen that the *cause* of the arrest, the arresting factor, is a sadly foreshortened sense of our desirableness, the loss of the child in us. So the story of Jesus is the story of the awakening of this sense by one who has it without the restriction called original sin, without that innate bad-mouthing of life whereby we are cursed.

Now our sense of our goodness can be awakened in two ways: indirectly and directly. All the awakening *of each other* that we do is indirect, that is, through the arousing of our desire for the other. You feel attractive in feeling attracted. Only God, by whose desire we are desirable, can directly touch our sense of our desirability.

Now the awakening effected by Jesus during his lifetime had to be an indirect awakening such as persons do for each other. But, Jesus being without sin and thus totally possessed of the sense of being desired by God, his influence was the maximum possible within the limits of person-to-person contact. The charm, the magic, the allure of Jesus swept the whole range of human interaction, exhausted the possibilities of mutual awakening. It created an entirely new hope for human existence – what he called the Kingdom of God. Precariously, it produced heaven on earth.

This totally new possibility for human living, awakened by Jesus in his community, was collapsed with his arrest and execution. And as it represented the maximum possibility for indirect interhuman awakening, its collapse meant there could be no revival at this level, no new leader, no new politics, no new human hope. To have been with Jesus meant a terrible loss of innocence in the way of mutual human expectation. There could be nothing *after* Jesus.

We may know what it is to have been so deeply entered and brought out by another person that the thought of starting again the labour of relating is intolerable. The special person is felt to have exhausted the possibilities, to have conferred on what would formerly have been exciting a dejà-vu quality. What if the person really *had* 'exhausted the possibilities', brought our life to its limits, taken us past all the landmarks, produced a real 'this or nothing' situation? What could follow such a person in our life? For the disciples, there could be nothing after Jesus.

Nothing, that is, except that *other* awakening that is the *direct* awakening of the sense of being desirable, by the One by whose desire we exist.

The experience on which the whole validity of Christianity depends is a series of encounters with Jesus after his death, that *effected* this direct, divine awakening, that gave the peace that is beyond all understanding, and thus showed Jesus to them *as* God in the flesh. There could be nothing after Jesus except Jesus as divine.

And because the whole social and political existence of people had been committed in this tempestuous train of events and had been plunged in the darkness of Golgotha, the new divine awakening touched that whole social and political existence and made of it the ekklesia, the God-called and Spirit-enlivened Church, the new humanity, the new polity of God.

So the release of our arrested development is not a private event, to be entered on by the mystic – though mystics do have a most important line on it and keep the hope for it alive – but a fully fleshed-out event in our history.

In the released condition, people know themselves for the first time. They know themselves as they come from the hand of God, desirable because desired. They know themselves no longer 'after the flesh', as defined by parents, race, culture, colour, class, sex, but in a new human focus which is cosmic. To them Paul writes: 'All things are yours, and you are Christ's and Christ is God's'. He tells them there is now no more male and female, gentile and Jew slave and freeman. There is only the new creature.

A student in my class, after I had explained this structure of indirect (or social) awakening and direct (or mystical) awakening, said, 'Isn't this symbolized by the cross? The indirect awakening is the horizontal beam, the direct the vertical.' This really shook me. I had always understood, in a general sort of way, that the cross

118

joins the divine and the human dimensions. But my student's insight was concrete and precise. Two currents are in synergy here: the life that flows from heart to heart and makes community, and the life that flows out of the heart of all existence. The horizontal energy reaches its maximum and explodes into the darkness of Golgotha, making way for the vertical energy to pour in and transform the earth. In the heart of Jesus, crucified and enspirited, both energies are one, the love of God trans-mystical, social, sacramental, the mystical made historical, the eternal word made flesh.

38.

Diagram of the transformation

(Start where indicated, and follow the direction of the arrows.)

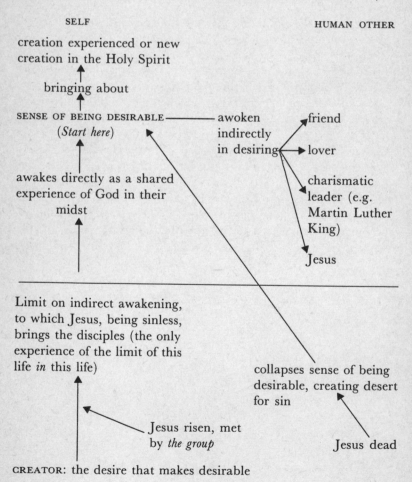

SELF

HUMAN OTHER

creation experienced or new
creation in the Holy Spirit

bringing about

SENSE OF BEING DESIRABLE —— awoken
(*Start here*)   indirectly
                                 in desiring

friend

lover

awakes directly as a shared
experience of God in their
midst

charismatic
leader (e.g.
Martin Luther
King)

Jesus

Limit on indirect awakening,
to which Jesus, being sinless,
brings the disciples (the only
experience of the limit of this
life *in* this life)

collapses sense of being
desirable, creating desert
for sin

Jesus risen, met
by *the group*

Jesus dead

CREATOR: the desire that makes desirable

Explanation

Some people like diagrams. They provide an opportunity to flash a complex argument from its left-brain habitat onto the screen of the right-brain. This one represents the central argument of this book: the structure of the transformation effected by Jesus in his first followers.

The sense of being desirable is awoken indirectly through desiring another. This happens on a wider and deeper (because more history-related) scale through the attraction of a charismatic leader.

Jesus, being sinless, represents the maximum in the way of indirect, social awakening. The horizontal dotted line represents this limits

With the horrible end of Jesus, the maximal awakener, the stretcher of life to its limits, all that indirect or social awakening can effect is exhausted and so breaks down, and a desert is created in which the only possible reawakening of the sense of being desirable is the direct awakening by the original creator desire.

The disciples experience this inward and total reawakening through a *shared* experience of Jesus as Spirit-giving. They see in *their midst* the power that the mystic feels *in the heart*. In other words, they see God. As doubting Thomas said, bringing the whole new experience to its climactic explosive affirmation: My Lord and my God!

In this experience, creation is experienced. The original power, that an immemorial dialectic of sin and disaster has rendered hugely problematic, shows itself to the heart as the loving one, the Abba of Jesus.

Conclusion:

Let This Mind Be In You

In this section, we move beyond the passion, death and resurrection as experienced by the disciples, as lived through by them, to consider the intention of Jesus himself, the 'mind' in which he embraced a wretched and horrible death. I have not attempted this transition before. It is only now that I have attempted it that I see how seriously incomplete is a salvation-theology without it. This section gives me the title for the present work.

39.

The chosen Passion (1)

The life that changed the lives of those it deeply influenced and, through their transformation, changed the world for all time, constitutes the greatest challenge to our understanding. What was the mind of Jesus? How did he see himself, his life, and its ending?

I have insisted, first and foremost, that we see that life *in its effect* on the disciples. How do we move from this perspective to the attempt directly to recreate the mind of Jesus himself?

This shift of perspective is a deepening of the perspective we are to advance beyond. 'Shift of perspective' is a bit misleading. For to become fully conscious within the perspective of my relationship with a person is suddenly to see *into* the person, to feel, as his or her motivating force, what I have hitherto known as a force in my life. So we might expect to find, in the reported experience of the disciples, something that suddenly opens the shutter on the mind of their leader and teacher.

Fortunately, a most precious evidence of this kind is available to us. It is the earliest known Christian hymn, quoted by Paul in his letter to the Philippians (Phil. 2:6ff.).

Now it seems to me that the most important, and the controlling thing, to say about this hymn is that it is a very early transcript of the impression produced by Jesus on his followers, of that 'impressing' as an ongoing drama of enthusiasm, disaster, and transformation. It is telling us that Jesus seemed to his followers like one who 'being in the form of God . . .' and so on.

Now this famous text has been interpreted for twenty centuries, and its opening words, 'being in the form of God', have suggested so beautifully the belief of our fully fledged Christology, that we have overlooked the fact that this very early testimony to Jesus must have been descriptive rather than doctrinal, must have to do with how Jesus was experienced, how people felt him.

The first step toward restoring to this text its original power is to realize, as many scholars have already done, that the descent, the self-reducing, that is being described is not the 'descent' of the pre-existent Logos into the flesh, but a descent, on the part of Jesus, into the horror and ignominy of the cross. The big question is: From what was this descent? It is years since I read the exegesis, such as it then was for a Catholic, and my only clear recollection is of *not* being clear as to the answer to this question. That 'form of God' bit was still tending to pull the whole thing back into the earlier understanding in terms of descent from the Godhead.

What was this 'equality with God', waiving his claim to which Jesus went to the cross? Logically it must entail *not* having to go to the cross. What was this 'divine entitlement not to die'?

Fr. J. Murphy-O'Connor maintains that this divine entitlement was sinlessness. To be without sin was to be 'in the form of God'. And to be without sin was to be not subject to death which was, in that anthropology, essentially the result of sin. It was because death was not necessary for Jesus as it is for us that he was able to choose it out of love for us, in a unique act of solidarity that, Murphy-O'Connor believes, is what Paul is thinking of when he speaks of Jesus' death as redemptive – this and not the idea of expiation.

Before we look at the fact that this anthropology is no longer credible, I want to say that this 'unique act of solidarity' has about it a haunting quality. Somehow *the chosen passion* is woven right into our Christian experience, liturgical, mystical, and political. There's something absolutely essential here.

And is not 'the chosen passion' of the essence of Jesus' pain-inducing self-presentation to the disciples? Are they not being pulled to Jerusalem by one bent on some awful end? Is not this intentionalism in Jesus precisely what disturbs the disciples and involves them in the drama? The first of this drama's three acts – of the contagion of Jesus extending their lives to the limit – is not merely *followed* by the middle act, the debacle. It heads insistently towards it. The chosen passion, then, was *Jesus as experienced by the disciples.*

My original contention, then, that the Philippians hymn must be seen as 'Jesus as originally experienced' is textually justified. 'The one who chose to die horribly' describes the man with whom the disciples had to do, with whom they couldn't cope. There is every evidence, then, for saying that the memory of a man whose horrible death was self-chosen *is* a memory, that it is *the* memory, the 'dangerous memory', that underlies and daily animates our liturgy

126

and prayer, that it is not something deduced from, and so dependent upon, the theory that a sinless person would not have to die. The rejection of that theory, then, does not render void the idea of the chosen passion, whose source is an indissoluble memory.

What this rejection does do is necessitate another conceptual structure that is at once consonant with our contemporary self-understanding and able to house the dangerous memory.

The desired structure is one that is implied throughout the present book. Original or generic sin is the arresting of our humanity at its Oedipal self-understanding, so that we take for reality itself and impose on society and on the universe *that* distrust of life, *that* self-repression, which was once appropriate when we were engaged on the business of becoming separate and sexually distinguished selves. In other words, we set our own limit on the meaningfulness of our life in our refusal to grow beyond the first stage. We build an invisible wall round our life. Outside that wall, uncharted by us, is death. For what does it mean to be ready for death? Who is? To be ready for death is to be living this life to the full, to its limit – which is death. We don't live this life to anything like its fullness. And what this means is that we don't believe in the glorious being that each of us is. Massively we repress the sense of our greatness, and our desires, in consequence, are weak. They reach their limit very soon, at least as regards innovativeness. We stay very near the known and the familiar. Thus we create a wall round ourselves, within which we live. And far beyond that wall is God's limit on us, death, the threshold of his loving embrace.

Thus the work of the Holy Spirit in us is twofold. First, the Spirit awakens our real desires that we have denied. Second, the Spirit teaches us to lose those desires in the huge movement of God in all that exists. We are to become, first honest, then cosmic.

Dante had a wonderful insight into this twofold necessity, of awakening and surrender. In Canto xxx of the *Purgatorio*, still accompanied by the vision of Virgil, he is met by Beatrice coming to him out of Heaven. Beatrice was the girl he had fallen in love with when he was very young. Seeing her, he feels again that love, and is afraid. It is too much for him, too much for the limited life he has made for himself. This is the turning point:

> The instant I was smitten by the force,
>   which had already once transfixed my soul
>   before my boyhood years had run their course,

127

I turned left with the same assured belief
   that makes a child run to its mot! er's arms
   when it is frightened or has come to grief,
to say to Virgil: 'There is not within me
   one drop of blood unstirred. I recognize
   the tokens of the ancient flame.' But he,
'he had taken his light from us. He had gone.
Virgil had gone. Virgil, the gentle Father
to whom I gave my soul for its salvation!

The experienced ambiguity between the Spirit's *awakening* of forgotten desire and the same Spirit's invitation to lose desire in God, runs through Eliot's 'Ash Wednesday'. And Eliot is Dante redivivus – at least as regards the poetry of what he himself calls 'the higher dream'.

What might it mean to stand on this promontory of the infinite silence, our consciousness not covered with the immemorially self-created membrane, our desire stretched to the full and thus brushed by that final dissolution wherein it will be one with the love that pulsates in all the universe? We can hardly know. But we can clearly say that the meaning of death for such a consciousness would be different, and that the difference would consist in the person being free in respect of death whereas we are not. And since we know in what our unfreedom consists, we can form some idea of the freedom. The unfreedom consists in the fact that death comes upon us as 'the forgotten limit', the ultimate crisis that our whole life treats as unimportant in the peculiar way that something repressed feels 'unimportant'. It is the unfreedom that exists between two strangers.

For the sinful condition that is ours, death is repressed (cf. *The Denial of Death* by Ernest Becker, one of the great books of our age), banished, 'queered', thrown outside the city. At the same time we know that this rejected status of death is the sign of our wretchedness, of our lostness, of an incapacity-to-feel that we cannot deal with. To meet with one who connected with, who befriended, who claimed, this our rejected death, would be to encounter an enormous and incomprehensible love. This love of us in our wretched unconnectedness, shown in the embrace of what we reject in horror, is intellectually nearly impossible to understand, but our deepest and simplest knowing moves out to it. At the heart of Christian experience down the ages, the uncomprehending sufferer stretches out to

128

the free, willing, understanding sufferer. And, thus outstretched, the uncomprehending sufferer can at last receive the communication of the incomprehensible *inflictor* as love, and see this in the fact of the victim raised from the grave.

Thus while there is not and cannot be an adequate theodicy or way of justifying suffering in a divinely ordered universe, the experience of our rejected death chosen in love by Jesus – dropped by us and picked up by him – radically alters the consciousness that makes theodicy impossible. That which makes of the natural disaster the manifestation of a heartless God is our own alienation of the disaster that is death. In the presence of the love that willingly enters this depth of ourselves that we have alienated, our eyes open anew to a once heartless universe.

This connection between our response to the insane inflictions of this world and the style of our consciousness has been brought to a hard focus by Paul Ricoeur. Vernon Gregson, in an unpublished manuscript, says: 'Ricoeur daringly but I believe truthfully suggests that only when we ourselves have achieved the capacity for offered suffering will the world not be too wicked for God to be good, and even then there will remain the little children . . .' And again: 'After Job, consolation will not do, only a new wisdom and a new transcendence.'

'The capacity for offered suffering' – that is the secret of the crucified that we are exploring. It implies a state of friendship with our deepest self that we alienate in repressing death, so that suffering is more than an affront. It is perfected and epitomized in Jesus. It puts him in that relationship to us sinful and death-alienating mortals which is experienced by the spiritually awakened as an overwhelming love. When Paul says, 'He loved me, and delivered himself for me,' he is speaking out of this first-hand knowing of the chosen passion. His statement does not *depend* on the anthropology that he *used*.

The same is true for his statement in Romans 5:6–8: 'Christ died for us godless ones. It is rare that anyone should lay down his life for a just one, though it is barely possible that for a good person someone may have the courage to die. It is precisely in this that God proves his love for us: that while we were still sinners, Christ died for us.' The core of the statement is the experience of being unjust and died-for; that is, of there actually *being* someone who befriended and chose that depth in all of us which we consign to oblivion and confront therefore as an alien but inescapable fate.

That is what being loved is all about – having cherished in oneself things that one dare not look at. The love of the chosen passion is experienced by the awakened soul as overwhelming and all-transforming.

What is fascinating in this connection is that according to Murphy-O'Connor Paul did not believe in the divinity of Jesus. He did not disbelieve in it. The conceptual structure in which Paul's experience of Christ would be more fully expressed by equating Christ with the Godhead had not, for Paul, shown up. All the more valuable, then, is Paul's vivid experience of Jesus as total transformer of life through his chosen passion and its glorious sequel. Through this conceptual limitation, Paul forces us to look straight at *a human self-determined life* as salvific, without shifting our focus to an incarnate God. The divine nature is not an ingredient in the mind of Jesus; it is the ultimate implication of a mind which, through the drama that it became, opened our eyes to the compassionate God in the face of his Son raised up from the dead.

We have much to learn from one who could see Jesus as totally transformative without equating him with God. Paul recognized what would later be called, correctly, the divinity of Jesus, as a human reality of solidarity and death-in-love. We need to recover the sense of *how* Jesus was divine, of the unique moral-psychological shape of Jesus – a need which is manifest in the striking fact that the more the Church today attempts to take a stand on justice and peace in our broken world, the more it becomes clear that the basis of that stand is either moral-psychological, either recognizable by Gandhi for instance, or mere words. Theologies of non-violence, of liberation, of women, are symptomatic of the need for that burning human centre. Theological critics who see only humanistic reductionism in these efforts are almost certainly without it.

40.

The chosen Passion (2)

The most important conclusion from the chosen passion has yet to be drawn.

We have seen that the repression of our original child sense of being all desirable, necessitated for our early growth but viciously perpetuated in all human societies, causes us to live short of our true limit, a living-short that is the root of the whole human offence to the planetary ecology. And we have seen that this self-placed limit leaves our real limit, death, 'out in the cold', always ambiguous, never integrated into our psychic wholeness, however impressively we progress in the latter.

Now the worst wound inflicted by this universal alienation of death is on ourselves as a universal community. The denial of our common fate makes of us strangers to one another. We see each other in the shadow of an unavowed mortality.

Thus the new penetrating love that overwhelms us, as the chooser of our common fate shines before us with the radiance of an at last visible divine compassion, makes us, in that encounter, one body. The sense of the one body is as primordially and preconceptually given as is the sense of the chosen passion and the divine compassion that it reveals. It is all one sense of newness.

It has still to realize itself as cosmic as well as social. It was the cosmos that was rejected in the great 'human arrest'. It is into cosmic existence that humankind is readmitted by the chosen passion. The Christ who, out of that unfathomable depth of sacrificial love, draws all to himself, is cosmic. Ancient Chinese wisdom understood humanity as the 'hsin' or heart of the universe. That position, that 'Stellung des Menschen im Kosmos', was denied in the human arrest. It was reclaimed by the first blood shed in total freedom.

The rejection of our common fate
makes us strangers to each other.
The election of this fate in love
reveals us as one body.
How much more truly than we know
do we call this choice the Passion:
life lived to the limit, and the limiting cross.
In this dangerous memory caught in the single word
we are one body cosmic.

41.

Communication in a dangerous memory

I suspect that not nearly enough thought has been given to the idea that Jesus had a consciousness greatly beyond the normal. I recall that J. G. Bennet discerned six levels of consciousness and placed Jesus, alone, at a seventh. But his approach is unusual. I think of Jesus as a quantum leap in human intensity, syphoned off into dogma. I am excited that Rosemary Haughton takes a very similar way, in *The Passionate God*.

The reason for our reluctance to go this route is probably the fear that it will lead to saying that Jesus is only more developed than others, not the unique person he is in Christian belief. But it is a curious way of thinking of Jesus' pre-eminence that dictates indifference to the factual impact of that pre-eminence on the ordinary run of humans – like asserting the presence of an earthquake not on the Richter scale. Christian belief depends entirely on what J. B. Metz calls a dangerous memory. Its massive formulas embody centuries of reflection on that memory, that original impact of one life on a few other lives, that has quite changed the world.

It has been believed of Jesus since the beginning that he was without sin. The late Bishop Robinson, a scripture scholar, used to remark on the fact that there is no record of this belief ever having been contested. We are more vulnerable morally than in any other way, so that anyone's goodness can be to some extent impugned. Yet no one, it seems, was able to do this in the case of Jesus. Iris Murdoch says that Socrates is the only other historical figure famous mainly for his goodness. Indeed his virtue was never impugned either. But then the claim to sinlessness was never made for him, a claim that *asks* for rebuttal, for someone to say 'Don't give me that! What about . . .?' In the case of Jesus, we have the extremely provoking claim, and silence on the part of the critics.

Now since sin was the early, pre-psychological name for the negative, anti-life, anti-growth tendency in us, and since our many schools of psychology have recognized in this tendency a matter of crucial importance, one who believes today that Jesus was sinless is making an enormous *psychological* assertion. He or she is describing a human psyche unimpeded by that huge inertial force that operates below the level where we distinguish between sins and mistakes, that deep reluctance to understand, to change, and to grow, that instigation of the flight from understanding. We shall have to exercise our creative imagination to fill out the description of such a psyche.

For about ten years now, I have been basing my Christology on the sinlessness of Jesus. But it is only recently that I have been able with the aid of this concept, to elucidate the central mystery of Christianity, the saving death itself. This has become possible because I have at last reached the beginning of an adequate concept of original or generic sin: a state of arrested development.

Sin, being evil, never fully reveals itself, its manner of working. We think we have caught it when we call it self-centredness. What we miss, by this description, is that self-centredness is essentially dependent on others for its satisfaction. One thinks of Osmund in Henry James' *Portrait of a Lady*, whose pride and disdain depend on the society he despises. Sin is in the implicit measure of the self by others, on which all the pretensions of the self are built. Sin is not a disregard for others: it is a misregard for others. It is a centring on myself *on the beam* of others. And the beam is not noticed – the failure to notice it being sin in action. Thus the socio-centrism, the anthropocentrism, of sin is never observed – until finally its effects reveal themselves in genocide in its many forms. What of course refuses, in its own interest, to reveal itself to us, is the self-contradictoriness in 'absolutizing myself in relation to others'. Evil *is* self-contradiction.

Now this state of arrested development, initiated in a partially flunked growth crisis, means that instead of our basic sense of the goodness and greatness of our life directing us to look beyond the human to the all-embracing mystery, our reduced sense of our goodness continues forever to wrestle with the socio-dramatic context never transcended. In this way we create our own limit for desire, the human world with its endless history of injustice and revenge. Far beyond this limit stands our real limit, death.

It is this gap between our self-created limit and the death that truly limits us that accounts for the impossibly ambivalent attitude we have to death. Who can make sense of the way we view death, of what death looks like to us? Who can find any coherence in this mixture of remoteness and unavoidableness?

Now a person without sin, a person free of our inbuilt self-contradiction, will not have this ambivalent attitude to death. This person's desire is powered by an unimpeded sense of his goodness, and so does not meander into the endless and immemorial human labyrinth. It reaches out to infinity, and acknowledges death as its only limit.

And how does this limit appear to our sinless one? Certainly not as the threat that death is to us who have defined ourselves short of it. It will not seem 'tragic'. It will not suggest the 'pompe funèbre'. On the contrary, it will signal the person's participation in a universe of death and birth. On the other hand, it certainly will not make the person's unlimited desire seem to no purpose. *That* message, of the ultimate hopelessness of it all, is the message of death to the sinful consciousness, a point that Shakespeare makes clear – though not to all – by having Macbeth, the man given over to evil, speak the famous nihilistic lines, 'Tomorrow and tomorrow and tomorrow'. Nihilism is the projection of the failure of our self-made, anthropocentric project *onto* death, charging the cosmos itself with our own failure.

On the other hand, the sinless person for whom life is limitless desire will see death as the gateway to new life *for desire*, as death is the gateway to new life at every level of being. Death will be the process that desire, to be all of itself, wants to surrender to. Desire, appropriated, finally intends a cosmic existence, to which death is the opening – but real death, not that weird spectral figure projected out of our sociocentrism, not the 'eternal laugh' that Valéry saw in the sunlight on his 'Cimetière Marin'. For the sinless person, death will be consummation.

But will this be a solitary consummation, something for oneself alone? At the level of consciousness we are trying to envision, the concept is quite incoherent. The question, 'What will become *of me?*', asked in respect of death, comes from within the citadel of sociocentric consciousness, so it is asked not of death but of the blurred death that we thence envision. For it is the conspiratorily willed remoteness of death that itself makes us strangers to each other and thus invites us to ask a solitary's question of death. The person for whom death, genuinely, feels to be consummation exists in a quite other relationship to all other persons. In this person the feeling, whose damming up separates us from one another and

135

from our death, runs free. *The same feeling* that senses death as consummation runs out to others whom fear withholds from this consummation and each other. For the sinless one, death is the consummation of his passion for humanity.

Paul, in Philippians 2, sees Jesus not merely as *accepting* death on the cross but as *choosing* it, the point being that, being sinless ('in the form of God'), he didn't have to die but chose to out of love. I have argued that we can, and must, reject the anthropology implied here, a naive conjecture on the prelapsarian condition, while maintaining, and entering more deeply into, the basic insight, the dangerous memory, of the man who died atrociously out of love for us, the person whose embrace of death as consummation and whose embrace of us alienated humans was one embrace. I would say that 'the loving choice of death by the immortal one' is an incorrect conceptualization of the basic insight into 'the loving death of the sinless one' or better 'the death of the sinless one as an act of love not of necessity'.

But the worst has yet to be considered. The worst is that it is as alienated from death, as enclosed in our self-made human enclave, that we see disaster as simply incompatible with a loving creator. One thing our terrible century is forcing upon theologians is unanimity concerning theodicy – that there isn't an adequate one. Thus the love of God cannot show itself in this world unless our fundamental numbness is thawed out. The thawing-out is effected by the resurrection encounters, the experienced divine endorsement of the compassionate death. The compassionate death is the human dimension of a mystery whose God-dimension is a self-identifying of God with the suffering of his creatures. The divine compassion shows itself in the raising from the grave of the one whom love for humankind drove to a horrendous death. It shows itself in this way as far more 'pathetic' than any speculation can conceive.

The urgency for 'recovering' the *consciousness* of Jesus is coming from the realization that only out of a new consciousness can a world on the brink of disaster be saved. I mean, that the search for the consciousness of Jesus is perforce a search within our consciousness. In its pursuit we are perforce hinting at a potential in our own consciousness. We are seeking within ourselves for that spark of reawakened compassion that blazed up in Jesus. In abandoning the christological chimera that I have compared with an earthquake not on the Richter scale, we are engaged in spiritual self-searching. And now that the Church, in its most visible form, is engaging in

136

the quest for peace and justice, it is becoming clear that the basis for this labour, if it is not to be a mere dogmatic formula, must be an existentially embraced style of consciousness and cognate action, a burning human centre.

That centre has shown itself on earth. It has only been able to show itself because it is in all of us, so that we can recognize it. Shown to us in a dangerous memory, it awakes in us the power to live beyond the city and to die for the city.

The centre is essential. We do not know how we are to save the world, but we do know that this is impossible save from this centre whence sin is swallowed up in life. Even non-violence is not enough, albeit it is far beyond where most of us have yet reached. But even non-violence leaves death unappropriated and evil thus still loose. For the non-violent person places the onus of his or her death on the inflictor, unless he or she can take the further step, the Jesus step, of appropriating his death in love for the inflicter and for all people.

These reflections have some application to the menace of nuclear annihilation. Robert J. Lifton, who has gone further than anyone in the psychological analysis of this menace, speaks of it as producing a psychic numbing. I would account for this numbing in the following way. Our style of consciousness makes death remote, and our whole bias is to keep it that way. Thus when new and strange historical circumstances bring death right up close, the only way to 'keep it that way' is to become, ourselves, numb in regard to it. This numbness is an accentuation of the lack of deepest feeling which is our 'fallen' condition. In its thrall, we are furthest from the redemptive, self-sacrificing stance. But this means, conversely, that the self-sacrificing stance is the only exorcism of the nuclear menace. The spectre and the sacrifice are mutually exclusive possessors of the human soul. At this end-time, in this twilight of 'scores of centuries', the crucified Logos and the deafening denial of all meaning confront one another in the fearful soul. There is but one way to throw off the demon of a new pervasive nihilism. It is 'to let that mind be in you which also was in Christ Jesus'. In that shared mind alone is eternal life – that eternal life whose natural symbol in the continuity of generations is swallowed by the image of mass-annihilation and planetary winter.

What we are about, in these reflections, is the recovery of a *subject* for the saving death, a consciousness in which death consummates a passion for humankind. This consciousness is beyond our rational comprehension, because it is within us almost too deep for our

137

recovery – almost, but not quite, and the 'not quite' is precisely that margin of us where we awaken to the dangerous memory. I have tried to express this in a poem, which I cite at the end. This consciousness, this subject of the new death in love, was at pains to impress itself onto that memory: for not only did he *undergo* that death: he *enacted* it, breaking the bread and saying, 'My body given!', and deepening the drama with the cup of wine as the spilled blood.

Unfortunately, just when we need its healing symbolic communication, the Eucharist is in poor shape – the worse for wear after twenty years of insensitive and uneducated experiment. We should be very open to the Spirit to show us how to find again, in the breaking of bread, that mind and that memory.

Finally, let me try to state the version of Lonergan's 'Law of the Cross' that is implicit in these reflections:

> Sin subjects us to death by making of it the triumphant alien, the final unmeaning, agent of an ambiguous God. Sin is taken away, therefore, by the embrace of death in love for us its helpless subjects, whose hearts can thus open to the unambiguously compassionate one.

I find it necessary to break down Lonergan's opening statement: Sin leads to death. In the logic of Lonergan's whole life-work, I have to see the drama of sin and death at the level of existential meaning rather than at the level of an ontology for which death came only with sin: the ontology of Paul and of that early hymn: an ontology whose abandonment does not make void, but invites us to deepen, the crucial insight to which it gave inadequate expression.

> I have a deeper soul
> that, to my surprise,
> is not surprised at injury or wrong:
> it prizes only life,
> to it, right is dead.
> Strive to live where life is:
> leave chosen anxieties.
>
> There is such room at this unvisited depth
> that no one would leave it for the world of right:
> strange castle, where the cells are liberty,
> the furnished rooms our prison.

42.

The oldest Christian hymn and a paraphrase

Though he was in the form of God,
  he did not deem equality with God
  something to be grasped at.
Rather, he emptied himself
  and took the form of a slave,
  being born in the likeness of humankind.

He was known to be of human estate,
  and it was thus that he humbled himself,
  obediently accepting even death,
  death on a cross.

Because of this,
  God highly exalted him
  and bestowed on him the name
  above every other name,

So that at Jesus' name
  every knee must bend
  in the heavens, on the earth,
  and under the earth,
  and every tongue proclaim
  to the glory of God the Father:
  JESUS CHRIST IS LORD!

(Philippians 2:6–11)

Being without sin, desire in him reached its true confines
so he knew death in freedom.

139

In this freedom he chose her at her worst,
her most abominated,
loving us, as lovers always do, where we abhorred ourselves:
he made her his whom we could not call ours

unless he wrested resurrection from her,
revealing the dreaded absolute power
as the compassionate one,
drawing us out of our corner of the universe
where we are captive of self-limiting desire
into our true being in his cosmic body.

43.

Jesus the verificator of myth

SUMMARY

In myth, the human soul voices, out of its mysterious depths, our yearning for transformation and new life. It does this in the form of a story of transformation. The encounter of the disciples with the risen Jesus convinced them that the great transformation had actually occurred and was occurring. This meant that the great myth had been verified, that we are living in a new age of realized myth. And this meant that in the attempt to understand the Christ-event in which this realization of myth is achieved, it is legitimate and even necessary to *consult* our deep mythic understanding of the laws of transformation. The point is that mythic understanding, having been validated by God in the resurrection encounters, becomes, if responsibly used, a guide to further understanding of who this Jesus is who has verified our myth of transformation.

The principal area where the Christian tradition has done this, has taken this hint from the new explosion of truth, is that of the human parenting of Jesus. Here we find that our myth of the Fall reflects our perception that parenting partly impedes, through the anxiety and horizon limitation of the mother, the coming of the child into full self-love as child of God, the implication is that one in whom this self-affirming was unimpeded so that he could carry through the massive historic verification of our myth of transformation, would have to have a mother herself freed by God from the narrowness of concern suffered by the parent. The thinking that led to the doctrines of Mary's Immaculate Conception was experienced by its practitioners as a logical necessity. What in fact was promoting it was a deeper and an elusive necessity: the necessity felt by mythic thinking validated by a prodigious event and urged to probe with new confidence the implications of that event.

Myths, I like to say, are the way we talked about ourselves before we learned to lie. They are stories in which the essential process of human growth and decline tells itself in a way that is beyond debate, holding up a mirror to ourselves. How do we make up these true stories of what it is to be human? What 'faculty' in us has this, as it were, direct view of our growing? What did William Golding draw on when he perhaps achieved, in *Lord of the Flies*, a myth? How does one tell the truth with that compellingness?

Whatever the answer to these questions, one thing is certain. *Without* this self-baring of the soul's essence, without this devastatingly honest story-telling, there can be no true religion. No myth, no religious truth. For how can we experience God, or share this experience, without there being stirred in us those depths where we most intimately know our plight, our tragedy, and our yearning for transformation and new life? People whose minds close down, almost visibly, when there is any suggestion of the widespread presence and spiritual power of myth in the Bible, are unwittingly turning away from those depths of the human soul in which God writes his story. Fundamentalism seems to me an instance of what the Bible means by 'hardness of heart', which is much more a blocking of *understanding* than the term implies in our contemporary idiom.

Bultmann's concept of demythologizing the New Testament is one of those rare mistakes that go so deep that to negate it is another mistake. What Bultmann is saying is that the New Testament is full of myth and we must cut through the myth to the existential core. The really important mistake here is a mistake that Bultmann shares with his fundamentalist opponents: a downgrading of myth in religious worship and life. He says we must get beyond myth. They say God has no use for it. The truth is that myth is indispensable if the deeper reaches of our being are to be touched and engaged and God's word to be heard.

Now let us look at the most vital of all our myths – the myth of transformation. The myth of transformation is rooted in the sense of the self as uniquely precious because intended by existence itself. As the whole thrust of life made conscious, the human self must perforce feel itself to be uniquely precious. The myth of transformation is that this essential personalized value will engage even death itself in its ultimate vindication.

Now the myth owes its vigour to this affirmative sense of self. So when the sense of self is inspired and inflamed, the myth of transformation will come into play. Lovers tell a story which comes 'out of the depths of the Celtic dream', as one critic described the myth of Tristan and Iseult.

Further, the positive side of self can be awakened in two ways: indirectly or directly. It happens indirectly through the interaction of persons. I sense my goodness *in* my desire for another and, more intensely, in that other's desire for me. The direct activation of my sense of my goodness can only come from the creative source of my existence. Then I know, I know not how, and with a certainty and happiness that I cannot explain, 'that existence is meaningful, and that my life, in sacrifice, has a goal,' as Dag Hammarskjöld puts it. We should bear in mind these two forms of the awakening of the self to itself in what follows.

Jesus was the man free of sin: free, that is, of that loss of intimacy with God and with the life in others and in all things which, the myth of the Fall tells us, is involved in our way of becoming self-aware. So there was a mysterious, all-embracing *contagion* at work in Jesus' relationship with his disciples. This contagion of the transcendentally free human being, this unique charm or allure of Jesus, awoke the sense of themselves-as-valuable in his followers to the maximum extent possible within the limits of personal interaction, of indirect awakening.

Now let us compare this awakening with that brought about in the depths of the soul by God, to which reference has already been made – the direct awakening. Clearly the direct awakening goes deeper, and thus triggers the myth of transformation and eternal life from a greater depth. But there is another point of comparison, which is *the* point. The awakening by interaction with Jesus, simply because it *was* an indirect or socially mediated awakening, tied the vigour and hopefulness, and hence the mythic celebration, of the awakening soul, *to history*, to the ongoing shared story of the people involved. It was *to life with Jesus* that the disciples consciously and continuously owed their enormously enhanced sense of self and ultimate destiny, the hope of the Kingdom.

Now with their hope of transformation tied in this unique way to the life of Jesus with them, the ending – and especially the shameful and atrocious ending – of that life was able directly to attack the hope enshrined in the myth.

This is something that never happened before. Certainly people had invested their deep myth-enshrined hope for life in charismatic leaders and in movements, but the investment could not be total because of the limitation, the sinfulness, of the leader. And so they never came to the point of head-on collision between the hope and the world's savagery. Thus the hope always remained intact, the myth ready to revive on some future occasion: and, when it did revive, be as powerless as ever it was to engage the power of the world to destroy its hope. With Calvary, the myth lost its innocence. Encouraged by the magic of Jesus to pit itself against all that this world could inflict, it fell flat on its face when Jesus, just like any other trouble-maker, was arrested, tried, and executed.

And brought to this pass, the disciples' hopeful sense of themselves and of life in them – this too was in a never previously entered place. Having been awakened to the maximum available to social interaction, thus to the maximum possible 'in this world', and then laid prostrate, it could only be revived by the direct mystical touch of God. The social, this-world life-resource was exhausted. There remained only the divine. Thus when they encountered Jesus newly alive and full of power and giving the peace that passes all understanding, they encountered and knew at first hand the power of God at work in and among them.

Most important, the new life they thus experienced had come to them as the sequel to the death they had been made to suffer. Here, then, was new life come out of that very reality of this world that the *myth* of new life, to keep its innocence, always dodges. New life came, not of the myth's 'hope springs eternal', but of the myth challenged by worldly reality and laid low.

And from that moment onward, the perennial myth of transformation and eternal life stood, not merely for something hoped for but for something that had been done. Some wise political thinker has said, 'What can be done is what *has* been done.' On this solid foundation, the myth of transformation has, since the first Easter, rested. It is a myth laden not only with human hope but with fulfilled divine promise.

And it is still a myth! It still moves, powerfully, in the depths of the human spirit. And what follows from its astonishing validation by Jesus is that the myth itself, and the deep awareness that gives rise to it, *is to be trusted* in our attempt most fully to appropriate the divine mystery enacted in us. The human person whose life and death has made of our deepest myth the word of God may be contemplated through the discipline of myth and thus further reveal his riches.

It is thus, I believe, that the Church, experiencing her Lord as the verificator of the myth of transformation, speaks with confidence

of the miraculous beginning of that miraculous life. Mythic understanding, validated by the risen Jesus, illuminates the genesis of
Jesus.

44.

Mary and myth

In urging upon theology the use of myth for the development of our understanding, I am anticipated by no less a figure than the father of modern psychotherapy, Sigmund Freud. It was in an ancient myth that Freud perceived his tool for a revolutionary advance in the understanding of the psyche. He used the story of Oedipus to devastating effect in laying-bare the process whereby the child comes to appropriate him or herself as sexually differentiated. Why did Freud use the myth for this purpose? Because it enshrines a fact of the maturing process that, until his death, never ceased to amaze him: that the human infant makes this final discovery in self-identity, the gender discovery, *dramatically*. Unlike all the other animals, who develop automatically and instinctually, we develop through a dramatic crisis in human relations, the three protagonists being the child, the mother and the father. It is thus dramatically, and traumatically, that one discovered oneself psychologically as a boy or a girl, stripped of an androgynous husk.

Now the real meaning of Freud's discovery is this. That at this crucial moment in the person's development, the process is in the hands of the key figures. They mediate it by their interaction, by the signals they give and receive. The child's psychological future is in their hands – and his of course, since he is one of the protagonists.

The discovery of the dramatic nature of our psychic growth is now being made for an earlier crisis than the Oedipal: our first crisis in fact, whose handling will affect all our subsequent times of change and growth. As noted earlier Margaret Mahler has shown that the infant's first and foundational sense of being separate from mother and thus individual is dependent, for its successful implanting, on a dialogue between mother and infant. At the extreme of unsatisfactory implanting, the infant may get the message 'Either be mine or be on your own!' – impossible alternatives that will give him/her a less than OK sense of separate existence.

146

Now let us, with the aid of myth, universalize Mahler's insight. Let us see whether myth does not reflect the perception that the awful moment of our becoming originally self-aware is fatefully in our own hands, with the implication that the alarming disparity between the mysterious nature of the event – nothing less than the whole universe come to consciousness as 'I' – and the limitedness and fallibility of the protagonists will result in something vital being lost in the process. The relevant myth here is the story of the Fall. And indeed it delivers – both as regards the dramatic, protagonists-dependent nature of the development, and as regards the tragic loss. Self-awareness, 'the knowledge of good and evil', comes into the man and the woman through a dramatic interplay. The woman listens to the serpent. She admires the fruit. She plucks it and eats. She hands some to the man, and he eats. And immediately their eyes are opened and they see that they are naked. The loss is powerfully conveyed. Sexual shame displaces the natural delight of a man and a woman in each other. The earth is no longer a circumambient paradise, and, worst of all, God is no longer a loving pervasive presence but a brooding, threatening power.

With this myth as our yardstick, let us ask a question: can the awesome process whereby the cosmos comes to individual self-awareness, committed as this process is to the exercise of a unique dialogic wisdom between mother and infant and demanding of both mother and infant, *ever* be carried through in such wise that the infant will emerge with a beginning of unimpededly self-loving separate existence? What then of the one we worship as Lord, God-in-flesh, because he towered above our human condition to the extent of being able to translate into certainty the hope enshrined in our timeless myth of transformation and eternal life? What of the source of a contagion that could stretch the hearts and minds of his followers to the limits of our worldly existence? Does not his birth and rearing have to have been such as to have laid the foundations for this new and terrible human freedom? And if in his final consummation he has rendered our myth trustworthy by making it God's word to us, may we not, *must* we not also trust our mythic understanding of our beginning to show to us the requirements for the birth and rearing of the Saviour?

We shall find that the scriptural account of the parenting of Jesus, whatever else is to be said of it by biblical criticism, exactly meets the myth-suggested requirements for one to be born into the freedom that the sinless Saviour is born into. For the myth of the Fall tells

147

us that the coming into self-awareness is in our hands *and thus* involves the loss we have referred to. Moving from the Fall-myth to the separation crisis of the infant, it becomes clearer why the mediation of consciousness involves this loss: the mother is bound to have preoccupations and cares of her own which to some extent prevent her from delivering the total message of love-supported separate existence to the new being.

And so the Scripture has, for Jesus, a Mother totally absorbed in the infinite purpose, and tradition has always seen this surrender of will at 'the one Annunciation' (T. S. Eliot) as foundational to the whole process of our transformation. The sinlessness of Mary is a very early tradition, for all the lateness of its definition by the Catholic Church. It has been evident to the myth-attuned mind of faith as it sought to extend our understanding of the luminous and all-transforming one back to his beginning. And what is especially fascinating is that the original understanding of Mary's virginity appears to have seen it *as* precisely this freedom from care and absorption in God which showed itself in the surrender of the Annunciation. The meaning of 'virgin' that Luke seems to be using is 'a woman *not belonging to a man*'. The woman without a care for herself, belonging to no man, and totally given over to the incomprehensible purpose behind all this universe – that is what a myth-attuned faith in the glorious cosmic Christ sees as his indispensable place of origin. The virginal birth and the Immaculate Conception are one in the perspective of a myth-attuned faith.

It may not have seemed to be a mythic consciousness made vibrant by faith that led to the definition of Mary's Immaculate Conception in 1858 – (an event which invited the disappointment and derision of a world tormented with the crises of the new industrial age). But what of the appearance, in the following year, of 'the Lady' to a peasant girl, saying 'Fear not! I am the Immaculate Conception', and what that led to? Rosemary Haughton sees Lourdes as revolutionary in the profound sense that it created a spirituality for the vast new industrial middle class. For myself, I feel much more at home with Lourdes, Fatima, and the recent apparitions in Yugoslavia warning of nuclear devastation, when I realize that an integral part of faith in Christ is a sense of realized myth that can open the eyes to 'the Woman clothed with the sun'.

So it is time to move Christology ahead with some new titles for Jesus. Jesus the miraculous life, the realizer of myth, making God cosmic in life as God is in myth: Jesus the anacosmetism of God.

148

And it is time to realize that by an understanding of myth that is essentially modern and rooted in one of the deepest insights of Freud, we are enabled to appreciate and appropriate the intuitive wisdom of the cult of Mary.

I conclude with another statement, from the *poetic* voice of modernity:

> There is the final addition, the failing
> Pride or resentment at failing powers,
> The unattached devotion which might pass for devotionless,
> In a drifting boat with a slow leakage,
> The silent listening to the undeniable
> Clamour of the bell of the last annunciation.

> There is no end of it, the voiceless wailing,
> No end to the withering of withered flowers,
> To the movement of pain that is painless and motionless,
> To the drift of the sea and the drifting wreckage,
> The bone's prayer to Death its God. Only the hardly, barely prayable
> Prayer of the one Annunciation.
>
> (T. S. Eliot, 'The Dry Salvages')

45.

Directed retreat: a turning point

I want to offer this retreat for world peace. Our culture at this time motivates through symbols, but much more by the symbolized technology that deadens, numbs the people to the very horror that it is preparing. A sense of evil here. Let this sink in to meet the love that holds us all in one. Let me, in so far as it is expedient, suffer this numbness that prepares us for slaughter, let me suffer for peace. Let me sink into the heart of Jesus as he dissolves in death for all humankind and all the world.

My director (henceforth 'B') says I am to ask especially for the grace to feel God's love for me.

FIRST DAY
Jesus: 'Believe in God; believe also in me.' When you let go at the centre of yourself, then I am, then you believe in me.
Self: I hear these words *in the context* of the part of me I don't want to talk about.
J: *I am* in my passion. So you cannot know me except in coming into *your* passion. I am your passion. Come close to me, come in closer. You've been in your intellect, making me intelligible there for students, for readers. Why won't you let me touch *you?*
S: I returned to *The Passionate God* – Rosemary Haughton's idea of some fundamental weakness as the place of 'passionate breakthrough', of the infinite's total bid to be itself in our flesh that must perforce secure itself in finitude. This corresponds well with the 'system' I have evolved, in which sin is the refusal to grow, to take the risk which tries to take itself, the infinite trying to be itself. During these days, my concern must be to take this to heart.
J: 'I go to prepare a place for you.'
S: I don't believe there's a place for me, for that thing I don't want to talk about. How do you prepare a place for me?

150

J: Only by dying in love, only by my dissolution into the embrace, in which I become who you are and invite you to become who you are.

S: So these two are connected: exposing my weakness that I dread to talk about, and letting you dissolve me in yourself. And yet in a way I talk very readily about myself – eagerly grabbing at the latest diagnosis of my condition, now the pre-Oedipal separation crisis. Yes, grabbing. This suggests that the diagnosis is an escape, a final cover-up.

J: 'You know the way there.' The way there is in yourself, in the dissolution in love which is your only possible response to the awful power to which life, once self-aware, feels totally subject, 'the power that cast us into the world to die' (Heidegger). I, alone, take that way – and so I *am* that way, *the* way. But you can't know me until you let this way open up in you. Believe in God – the power. Believe in me.

S: I must confess to a certain allergy to John's gospel. I don't have the link right between my image of a Jesus of history and him who is the way. Which is why, of course, I have devoted my whole theological life to establishing their identity! Has it seemed so necessary to establish this intellectually *because* I'm not letting 'the way' open up in myself?

('The historical Jesus' – what a monstrous ambiguity this phrase conceals, suggesting that these two are one: the Jesus who actually lived and, like all who have lived, is part of our present; and that very small part of this Jesus – as of any other person of the past – that can be established by strict historical method. Treating the historian's Jesus as the historical Jesus is one of the greatest scholarly arrogances of all time. We would never treat our great-grandparents this way.)

S: But I can't, absolutely I can't, 'take that way' by myself. I must let you take it for me. That is the mystery. Only this strange one who *alone* once took this way of chosen dissolution can bring me to that place in myself where *alone* I can recognize him.

(And who is the further away from this understanding: the liberal theologian or the fundamentalist? Both are out of sight of it.)

A character in A. N. Wilson's *The Healing Art* had been struggling all his life with images of his own making – the only thing one does struggle with in this way of trying-to-get-free. I identify with this. It's the intrapsychic other, who is no other, who for that reason holds one in a stranglehold. I want to open this to you, *the* other.

151

From the intrapsychic other to the healing other. How does this feel? How do I feel this? Let me pray this wordlessly.

The pre-Oedipal personality is beset with intrapsychic others, with a forest of personal symbols for the other that never get to *be* other, since one never got to be separate. B says this was Jung's struggle, magnificently carried through on the edge of madness. My Jesus-other has been strongly intrapsychic. It is not so much the *Jesus of history* that has been my obstacle to grasping the Jesus of faith. Rather it is the intrapsychic, narcissistically projected Jesus that has been the obstacle to the coming-to-be in me of the Jesus who is surrender to 'the power that casts us in this world to die', the Jesus who alone grapples with the evil in life from which the narcissist forever screens himself. Let me pray now this new association of Jesus with maturity, with openness to death.

Looking back to John 13, I notice how intimately he weaves the theme of 'love one another' into the centrepiece of Jesus' self-manifestation. With Jesus self-manifest, *all* the others pass from the intrapsychic into the real people to be embraced. We stop knowing people 'after the flesh'.

Is my new idea of original sin an extrapolation of my own struggle with the intrapsychic other? Does the non-separated have an insight into the never-completely separated?

How does this differ from Bultmann who reduces faith in Jesus to existential self-exposure? Absolutely, I feel. Bultmann's picture is individualist. Jesus for me articulates the community of history, forever drawing together those whom he liberates from themselves.

B *comments*:   Things you have helped others to, have still to happen in you. There is some resistance. You have the sense of running away. Try the Prodigal Son. It is good to *understand* the escape – I'm saying something important here – but I'm concerned that your attempt to articulate it can sidestep it. Understanding will come later. Now *acknowledge* the escapist tendency in yourself. Bring this back to him. Return to the Father *with* all that. Tomorrow is the day for confronting sinfulness, in prayer, as wordlessly as possible. Pray to know the depth and immaturity of your own sinfulness. Taste it. Your writing enables others to taste – you have still to taste. Let yourself experience what you have enabled others to experience. Your sin – don't seek to *name* it. Don't intellectualize it. This could be a trap, escape from the grace he wants to give you.

The indecent association of you with my sinfulness. Your willingness to be in the place where I am not willing to be, where I am not willing.

My whole intellectual operation converges on your desire making me desirable. I ask to be able to appropriate this. There is somewhere in me where I don't want you to come. I don't have to ask why, that's not the point. I only have to acknowledge that place. Only that. And I don't have to find the genetic roots of that weakness.

J: Be in that place, then I'll be myself for you. Only in that place can you receive my death-in-love, my awful Godhead. Only in that place am I no longer in double focus, historical–theological.

S: What is my way of being within the human citadel, untouched by death, untempted to God-denial? I know it well, G knew it well – 'Sebastian moves slowly through life!'

The Introit for this evening's mass was: 'I am the beginning and the end of all things, I have met death, but I am alive, and I shall live for eternity.'

SECOND DAY

I dreamt last night that I was just about to be crucified, trying to imagine what the pain would be like as the nail went into the wrist. I've dreamt this before, and of being under sentence of death.

Being crucified is the alternative to letting myself be crucified-for, to letting God love me, to letting God *be* God in Jesus in me. Taking a deep breath and letting this be. Walking over the viaduct after last night's session, I felt momentarily this enormous gentleness. The idea of what I had to do seemed unwelcome, somehow distasteful and threatening, as B proposed it; it became sweet soon after on this walk. I've known this sequence before.

The other pole of this letting God love me is the coming into one focus of Jesus as God, is the emergence of the real as opposed to the intrapsychic-versus-historical Jesus. Thus being loved by God and being crucified-for are the same.

Then came the realization that to expose myself to the loving of God will involve the falling-away of layer upon layer of covering of the wound of emptiness, the wound of not-being-anyone satisfactory, going right back to childhood.

The point of insertion for evil, and indeed for the Evil One, is

153

this inner sense of not-being-anyone-satisfactory. In the early days at Downside, I used to speak of a sense of being insubstantial.

There has also been in my life much sense of fullness, a sense of inner being that other people didn't seem to have. I attracted, and was attracted by, another monk who had it, and we spoke of it.

These two opposites are quite compatible, I feel. One thing that stands out is that the sense of fullness, of my life being exciting, came entirely and only from contemplative prayer.

I do not let God love me because I do not love myself. This is quite different from saying that I need a God to love me because I do not love myself. The obstacle to God's love cannot be the same thing as what calls out for it.

Point of entry. I would find the point of entry.

The inner nothing is not the void that God fills. It is the failure to be of the being that God loves.

I recall the valuable discovery of Langler, that some young people took readily to self-dissolving meditation because they didn't like themselves. The trap of premature mysticism.

Rosemary Haughton says the most dire result of sin is the separation of spirit and matter. Surely the origin of this separation, in a person's life, is that *this* matter, this body, this life, feels unspirited, empty of meaning. Error originates in bad feeling. 'For the water of regeneration and the blood of the new covenant came – both, and both together – from the passionate death of the human being, Jesus, and must always find their origin there, or fail in their power to save.' (*The Passionate God*, p. 169)

The parable of the Prodigal Son caused tears, and repeated the lesson of my retreat five years ago: that I took the Father's property, given to me in mystical experience at Downside, and spent it on myself, on building around myself the world that prayer experience had introduced me to. This failed – farcically. The relationships built on mystic expectation only served to expose the inner emptiness that prayer had been the relief from. There was famine. And in so far as the famine is felt, the emptiness returns ('returns' is the right word here, suggesting a gnawing recurrence) but – and here is the trap – the emptiness is not the void that only God can fill but is the original, early not-being-anyone-satisfactory that *repels* God's advances. Thus the son's first reaction to the famine is self-loathing, which the father hastens to swallow up in indulgent love.

'Your brother has come, and your father has killed the fatted calf, because he has him back safe and sound.' That has always moved me. The father's concern is so completely different from the son's tortuous thoughts about himself and what he calls his life – it is simply that the boy *is well* and that 'he has him back safe and sound'. This simple delight of the father is so difficult to receive in a life that has been built on the feeling of *not* being so good, of its not mattering if one *is* safe and sound. Uncovering the substantial reality that God cares for, being the creator, is the point.

Dissolution in the love whereby I am: dissolution in the nothing I feel myself to be. These are the polar opposites of our experience. And, like all polar opposites, they can look terribly alike. An experience of dissolution, coming violently and early, can go either way, can fasten on either our nihilism or our yearning to be swept up in God.

   – Yet when we came back, late, from the Hyacinth garden,
Your arms full, and your hair wet, I could not
Speak, and my eyes failed, I was neither
Living nor dead, and I knew nothing,
Looking into the heart of light, the silence.

                    (T. S. Eliot, 'The Waste Land')

How can I believe in the joy of God *in me*, in this exiguous existence, this endlessly apologized-for me? I remember once visiting Downside as an alumnus and one of the monks, a jovial innocent creature, asked, 'Is this just a surprise visit?' Whom could I 'surprise' pleasantly by turning-up?

The parable is revelation to me. 'Against you alone have I sinned.' I have closed myself off from you, jealously guarding my secret emptiness. Nothing is so jealously guarded as nothing. There were the daring sorties into life. But there was ever the retreat, back to the safety of not feeling all well. I guess safety is a most important value for me. It is where I oppose the great saying, 'He who would save his life will lose it.'

It's a question of *finding* my point of refusal, rather than of naming it. But surely finding means naming – descriptively, or better connotatively.

Where there is no ego, evil has an easy entry. Where ego is weak, evil has an easy entry. For ego has supergo and id with it, that is, some hook-up to the larger-than-myself. Kurtz, in Conrad's *Heart of Darkness*, is hollow at the core, and so is drawn into the heart of darkness.

155

I ask to be shown how to open my heart of darkness, my heart of concealment, my heart of secrecy, my heart.

B *comments*: Keep on with the Prodigal and Psalm 51. Also Ignatius' second meditation. Pray to be shown your point of refusal and his embrace.

NIGHT

After talking with B, something became very clear to me. I always do the following: present a picture of myself as paradoxical, and *ask the person*, 'How d'you think that fits together? Explain me to myself!' Why do I do this? To shift responsibility from myself to the other person. To put myself down, presenting myself as an object to be dissected. Somehow I treat myself like a little girl treats her doll – put it in the pram, tuck it up, take it for a walk, toss it around in the company.

It came to me very strongly in prayer that I shall never again in this way propose myself for another's explanation. I am my own explanation. I act, however stupidly, out of me. *I* act.

The person that I am and act, that is unique and me – I prayed, very intensely, just to *be* this person, not hawk it around or offer it for dissection. This person, uncomplicated, unsecondhand, ungeneralized, is whom *you* are addressing.

To make my self-understanding dependent on another's explanation is to behave as though I were any object – in the case of an object, judgement depends on coming to understand it. But who *I* am *precedes*, for God's sake, any analysis by myself or anyone else.

Is not sin this alienating of myself? This unworthing and hiding of myself. Sin is hiding from you who want *me*. Sin is the cover-up of the unworthed. 'Tell me who I am and why I behave as I do!' is the voice of self-displacement, the sin, of hiding, above all of denial of my unique responsible existence.

THIRD DAY

There is a point where awkwardness becomes refusal, where wonkiness becomes wilful, where sickness repels the healing hand. My aim must be, not to define sin but to find my sin.

I was given a clue in a dream last night. I am at Downside (dammit, so much of my dream life is at Downside). The whole community, vested for Mass as I am, is dancing – especially I notice

156

the ones I wouldn't expect to be dancing. One or two say, 'Come on!' I say, feeling very awkward, 'No, everyone's tired by now.'

Sin is where I want to be impersonal rather than be absolutely and ultimately personal. Where the awkwardness takes that funny turn. William Golding, in *Darkness Visible*, has his characters who turn evil attracted by 'the weird'. Internalized weirdness perhaps. Internalizing the weirdness that others see in me. The *point* of sin is the point of grace's entry.

I cannot find the 'no' in my life unless you *to whom* I say 'no' show yourself, make felt your touch. I can *locate* the 'no', in a certain awkwardness that I have got used to, symbolized-to-feeling by the dream in which I decline to dance. But that is only the location of a more mysterious denial, a settling for being without life, a settling for isolation. The point where 'sore' becomes 'sour'. The point where I must recall what ancient liturgy says of the Holy Spirit: Quoniam ipse est remission omnium peccatorum – for he is the remission of all sins.

Doing the Exercises, I chose to identify very strongly with a young devotee of the rabbinate who was filled, I imagined, with dread when the man with the withered hand broke in on the liturgy and, far worse, got Jesus' attention. It was my 'awkward' streak that was touched, and this proved a, perhaps the, turning-point. It revealed itself as a being scared of where I cannot feel – which turns out to be a being scared of the feeling below the surface at just that point.

But none of all this articulates the movement, the surrender, that *you* require – tomorrow I shall want to alter this word to 'instil' – *at* that point. Why do I suddenly think of Jung's inability to bring his forehead all the way to the ground in that dream. I really identify with that. I know *where* and *whence* the jump is. But the jump remains untaken.

Should I think of the jump you, Jesus, took from this solid world into the power that showed only as the cross? That feels much too grandiose. My first jump must be much more intimate, more 'singular' to myself. Much closer to that 'awkwardness'. I have to feel and know and repent *my sin*, my innermost desire to go it alone, my stoic way.

I read the parable again. Nothing came – except a much closer association of the famine with my Liverpool and early American experience where my spiritual wealth ran out and I met deep desolation. Conversion came with the long retreat, but it left me

157

very smug and absurdly over-confident in my giving of the Exercises to students. The deep root of sin was still unsounded, I now think. There has to be a hatred of sin. The almost unavoidable confusion of this with self-hatred is what makes real conversion so difficult and rare. I ask, boldly, for just this saving grace.

> Let slip your hands within my rigid self,
> my body you find one with what I call
> soul, and make its jailer till *you* come,
> logos all flesh, spirit all life releasing.
> You who forgive unlife, being life-yourself,
> anticipate me who cannot repent unlife,
> only wrongdoing, only unlife's symptom
> until you come upon me, so I hate in me
> only unliving – but that most intensely.
> I must await in patience for some sign
> that you indeed have touched the tender spot,
> the sore that soured to ingenuity
> to fashion life without you, hiding the absence.

AFTERNOON

A new sense of you as the absolute, 'pure will' dimension of my repentance/surrender. *You* forgive/unleash/release. You alone, out of a mind not mine, in no wise to be simulated. Creator you. A. E. Housman, homosexual, asked 'Why did you shape me so ill?' This denied that you were shaping him, trying to shape him, at the moment. Forgiveness gives shape into the future.

B *comments*: You turn away from 'the jump taken by Jesus'. Why? That's what your first book is *about*! That dream of being crucified could indicate your being drawn this way. Get a sense of the beautiful ambiguity of all these messages.

Dwell *in* wonkiness as you focus on Jesus crucified. Against resistance, which would *be* the wonkiness. Take any one of the Passion narratives. Concentrate on him, with room for intense love, as he endures crucifixion that you might come alive, and have sorrow for your refusal of the healing hand. I can assure you that this works. I learned it from your first book. You have said in *The Crucified Jesus is no Stranger* that one's refusal of the healing hand comes to clarity in contemplation of the crucified. The evil in you, the refusal of the healing hand, is dramatized in the crucifying of Jesus. (I reflect,

158

though, that in *The Crucified* I don't yet see sin as refusal of the healing hand. I see it anthropologically, existentially, in the manner of Ernest Becker, not yet personally.) Concentrate on the Passion. Your dream of death sentence by your English community *also* suggests you associate with the crucified. Ambivalence is important. *Whenever* (Listen!) you look at your wonkiness only with the 'hermeneutic of suspicion', you put yourself down and that *is* the wonkiness accentuating itself. Others see positives in all your victimhood where you see only negatives. You find it very difficult to trust that the symbols are ambiguous.

This dogged insistence on a hermeneutic of suspicion *is* your wonkiness becoming wilfulness, to which you have referred. Pray to trust that all has happened for your good, as in Romans 8.

Freud operated in a world saturated with false consciousness, and so had to promote the hermeneutic of suspicion. We, on the other hand, are saturated with negativity about ourselves.

The very emphasis on negativity dodges the reality of sin. You might look up what Paul says about that thorn in the flesh. The message is, 'Why should I take it away? I've been using it all these years to bring out the person you are'.

FOURTH DAY

I woke at 4.30, and knew a corner had been turned. I got up and went down to the chapel. The following 'rhythms' are the attempt I made to articulate what was moving inside me:

> Thank you for dying for me
> thank you I can at last say this
> thank you that just where I
> endlessly try
> the old escape
> into self-rape
> and *will* not cry
> you, loving, take
> my old mistake
> my ancient hate
> upon yourself, and
> die up on a cross for me.
>
> The first thing I saw
> and wrote about

was the last thing to feel.
The next thing is to remember
all the times
all the times
of escape into self-downing
all the time
all the time
that way alone
ever prone
my awkwardness to flee
and finalize
all this, enormous folly
you swallow in the chosen Passion
of a love that, God-unfettered,
dies for me.

For centuries they said
'It's all been paid.'
Not paid but swallowed rather
in the simple passion of a God
who can take into an infinitely receptive heart
dissolves the divide between our pain and pleasure
into a love that says
simply let me have all
let me absorb into my flesh with nails
the self-contempt that finalizes sin
makes it forever, hell.
Can you at last look at my bleeding
not as adding (and never sincerely,
never quite able to believe me God)
to your guilt but as swallowing it in my delight in you
whom indeed *I* did make
who can at last believe I did?
The cross that free from *this*,
so heavy, so relentless, so always,
is without strain to faith
the cross of God.

Thank you God forsaken man
for bleeding wounds and gravelled pain
are your divinity for me

who feel you just where I would flee.

How easily you take me now
how easily you now are God
in catching me, whose subtlety
disguised my flight in make-believe.

Jung's dream:
The head bowed
touching the stone
the moment of contact
makes Jesus God
and me inalienable.

I can lie on the couch of your dying
hardly knowing myself in rest
not yet quite sure, having to look continually
at you crucified who only yesterday
seemed a pious ritual:
as I came out of sleep
you were for most real
you were a rhythm in my heart's breathing
which said:
Just where I,
just where I . . .
you who die,
you who die:
between these limbs of litany
the bridge formed and firmed
and I could thank you
for the first time in my life I swear
simply, for dying for me.
And I must wonder how others get with such ease
to this love-bewildering proposition.
And can I join them saying yes to what is in their eyes?

This is not the answer to everything:
it is the answer to me.

Sin holds off the healing hand,
preferring to condemn itself

and hide itself in condemnation.
The protracted, repeated hiding
swells the disgrace of sin
which, being disgrace,
must be seen as loathsome,
cannot be seen as it is
nothing, dis-grace.

There will be fewer surprises
in the world out there:
the liberated heart
does not look askance
on the follies of men and women.

The fled-from is myself.
Who knows what could happen
when the flight stops?
It will take time for it to stop though,
the inertia gone out of it.

You unravel in your flesh
my tent of flesh to keep me in:
so I go free, eternal me
leaving behind the flopped tent of sin.
'The river's tent is broken.' ('The Waste Land')
'There is freedom from a burden that I carried.' ('The Family
Reunion')

Freedom to walk at last without the accustomed weight on my back.
A simple line drawing, in *Good News for Modern Man*, of the cross,
and men walking up to it with heavy bundles that vanish as they
walk on from this meeting. I wondered subconsciously, 'Could this
be true?'

Late in life
template of my times
con-template open yesterdays
which run together
into one now
the body changed to history's exchanging,
no longer this flesh closing
to the wound of rejection

to cover a wound of rejection
to cover a wound of nothing
but open now, wounded now, absorbing now
absorbing now in love
in which, my burden vanished,
I stand light
and breathe all those wretched times
of late, of awkward, of seeking to palliate
in others by flattery
the emptiness.

The Scripture must be fulfilled. Gethsemane. My whole christological search has culminated, intellectually, in the deliberate Passion, the chosen Passion, far far beyond the accepted Passion. Philippians 2:7 remembers above all the *choice* of 'the form of a slave' and the slave's death.

Now I am appropriating this, I feel. The first instruction I received, early this morning was to *thank* him for dying for me. We only thank for something willingly done, done by choice.

It probably is not possible to account rationally for the relief experienced in contemplating the chosen Passion. There is just the sense: there had to be this choice if there was not to be numbing and freezing into hell, there had to be this choice, and it had to be a choice, and it had to be the awful suffering of humankind in which we see, dramatized on a sickening scale, our desperate self-oppression.

The narrative does not portray a victim in the common sense of total passivity to unmanageable events, but an agent acting in response to an accepted personal destiny. In *this* vision is the 'relief from a burden that I carried'.

In Jesus crucified I see what I am refusing in refusing to let God's love untangle me and be itself *in* my awkwardness untangling. Refusing the untangle, I tangle vigorously, strangle and crucify myself. Self-crucifixion is the final unfreedom undone by *chosen* crucifixion, the ultimate freedom of the spirit in the flesh. And the choice of crucifixion is the choice of me. The chosen Passion makes a chosen People.

'But he gave him no answer, not to a single charge, so that the governor wondered greatly.' In the synoptic accounts, from the moment Jesus is in the hands of the civil power (of life and death) he has nothing to say for himself. Only John gives a dialogue with

Pilate – for John's gospel is built with dialogues. The silence of the victim is the clarity of the victim as self-directed.

The awkwardness (that's the preferred name I'm now giving to the sore centre) takes off into rhetoric like an arrow from a taut bow. I am learning, of the crucified, to reside in the awkwardness, of the self-surrendered to rest in this otherwise impossible place. This is the first lesson in true self-loving. It comes entirely from the bleeding hands and feet. It is true rest, true centredness.

This is the healing of memories. For I learn to *be* where the wounds are. 'By his stripes we are healed.' How did Isaiah know this?

The greatest rest is to rest where no rest has ever been – in the awkwardness, the wonkiness, the woundedness, the fleed-from place. How on earth did Waugh know to call his character 'Sebastian Flight'? A case of what David Tracy calls the uncanny.

My abiding love for Eliot is explained. It is coming to be recognized that Eliot wanted to give people access to their deep, strange, fearful, power-laden images below the level of decent awareness. Whatever you remember, I say now to myself, don't move off it into 'what might have been'. 'What might have been points to one end that is always present.'

B *comments*:   Have you *said* it – 'Thank you for dying for me'?
Resting is allowing the healing hand to enter.
Stay there!
Let the drops of blood fall on the wounded self.
Rest there for years.

THAT EVENING
Walking slowly along the busy streets, the new resting-place, nesting-place forming in my heart, it came to me: Now that I am at rest, or rather have a position of rest, the future with death in it falls into place. I am no longer doomed to fly, as though I will never die, until meaninglessly I drop.

The sore, sick, awkward place is vast, I find. It has room for all the wretched of the earth. That sounds grandiose, but it is not. The saint is one who *acts* on this feeling of the heart as universal asylum. Once you *stop*, the world looks wildly different. Liberation theology talks of stopping, to experience the utter powerlessness of the poor, no transport, no life-facilitating technology, sheer slow.

164

Creator-terrible what do I know of life, of cannibalism in extreme circumstances, etc.? This was a strong prayer feeling.

Last night's dream. A young man, tall and dark, with his back to me, makes the sign of the cross and stoops down, picks up a huge piece of dung and puts it in his mouth. He turns, his mouth open so I see the dung inside. I am strongly repelled.

Associations. Young man, sex symbol, strong escape symbol, eating dung forces me to pause, to stop my flight into his illusory embrace. He signs this action with the holy sign of the cross, of Jesus bleeding holding me unmoving in my wonkiness. I was going to write 'in the stillness' – O that Eliot stereotype! – which suggests calmness and peace. But the rest in wonkiness is not that – as regards coming into it. The way in is the way of blood. I am repelled by the image of 'letting his blood drip on my woundedness'. I ask for the grace of an absolutely plenary head-on meeting with the physical awfulness of the crucified, however that is to be imaged into symbol. I *know* there is an element of *repulsion* that runs through my whole affectively as regards the wounded Jesus, cannibalism, dung, intense warmth between people, mutual grooming of animals. This came up during the long retreat.

To forgive is to get behind the offence. To accept forgiveness is to let behind the offence, to admit the healing hand to that place within, which is not bad but – worse from my point of view – helplessly incoherent and to-be-fled-from. I have to surrender to Jesus' Passion reversing the hardening of the soft centre. I notice that in talking to B the soft centre is more embarrassing to talk about than my sins. I notice that I hate being asked – especially by women – about my life's motives, why I came to the States, etc. It's the wobble I'm protecting – from them and, in the end, from Jesus wounded.

In prayer. I'll pay *anything* to be touched there and set free. You paid *everything* to touch me there. Let love join these two in one deal.

The old meditational 'Quis, quid, cur?' (Who suffers? What does he suffer? Why does he suffer?) worked.

I can't give myself theological permission to kiss the pierced feet – I mean, the kiss does not attend on theological permission. Theology *follows* on the kiss. All my writing perhaps has been a quest for theological permission for this indecent intimacy.

There is no tête-à-tête with Jesus from the position of post-

Cartesian flesh-enveloped privacy. The only, and all-embracing intimacy, is letting Jesus *be* Jesus, be the love that burst open death and embraced the whole world.

I feel that these days are bringing to a crisis my whole relationship to my writing. Brought out by the fact that the 'poetic' stuff that came out of the encounter with Jesus was heard by B as spoken to him *rather* than my telling of the encounter. The writing that has helped a lot of people, including B, is also the *armour* that I have formed around the wonk or whatever.

B *comments*:   One of the most important areas to appear is the non-correspondence of your theology with your experience.

'This is your hour, and the power of darkness.' An hour of very deep contemplative prayer, with sort of flashes or intervals of Jesus crucified. I couldn't say anything, not because I was holding back but because in these moments saying would break whatever is going forward. If anything he was 'saying' me. I had a will to be enveloped by him.

This experience is not new to me. The difference now is that there is opened up to me *my* 'singularity' or awkwardness – whose oneness with all the poor of the world is being felt more today (the fifth day). I do not forget the young man eating dung. I am beginning to register it as a necessary, necessarily violent balancing image for me, I mean violently associating the escapist vision with the escaped-from self.

J: Join me in being crucified for your community – for a change, instead of interpreting all those execution dreams as my judgement on your frivolity. Let dream images be ambivalent. *Anything* to get you *with me*. Anything. I love you. I want you. I am drawing you. Why won't you let me do this? Why *always* the elaborate, sometimes beautiful, aesthetic defence against me?
S: Yes Jesus, I want to give way entirely to your drawing near, near, near. I offer up to you, for your transforming, all my sophistication.

I have repressed dangerous feeling, numbed myself at danger spots. A woman I was very closely involved with told me this.

Dung! it doesn't matter! Dung! it doesn't matter! One of those contemplative rhythms that seem to let in light.
J: Let me come to you, get near you, draw you to me. I love you.

166

I am love with all power. You have nothing to fear, and nothing to lose except what you want above all to lose.

S: Yes, I'll come to you. I can feel the resistance in me crumbling. It could *never* crumble till I felt, refelt, recovered, my wonkiness. My place of poverty, all the world's poverty. That's what I have to give, I now realize. Rosemary Haughton's 'weak spot', the point of breakthrough.

B *comments*: The insight into your 'armour' is important. Your offering to Jesus of all your sophistication is your version of Ignatius' prayer, 'Take O Lord and receive, all my liberty, my understanding and my will.'

Stay open to that new insight into world poverty.

That dream of the young man eating dung could be your resistance to me holding you to the repulsive image of the blood falling on your woundedness. This doesn't deny your interpretation. Ambivalence again.

Your writing will become less of an armour as the 'citadel' gives way.

Stay just where you are now, repeating your last meditation.

NIGHT

J: My blood struck from my body as it meets world resistance to the love of which I am made, as it flows over you, reverses the direction of your outward movement. You move out of inward, fearful softness to form a hard shell. My blood turns this tide in you, back to your soft, dreaded centre. I love you. That is, my life seeks yours, as only happens with lovers. A lover will sometimes say, 'Love you!' leaving out the 'I'. Doesn't that embarrass you when you recall it. It is the most brazen thing a lover shows. 'Love you' means 'I want to see you loving yourself.' Indeed I want this for you. I want to see in you the effect of my bleeding love.

S: You shall. Now that I feel the pulse of your loving in my wonky centre, now that the flow is in me, I for the first time ever love myself. I love myself whence only sin could come until your dangerous love, released in blood by world's refusal, got in there.

J: I love you. I am you. I demand, with love's urgency, that you consent to me.

S: I do consent, that you love me where I never let anyone come.

Once 'the thing' is loved, it can be looked at, understood more.

167

Standard reactions to situations with persons, hitherto quite reflex, invite scrutiny.

SIXTH DAY

I have to rewrite Lonergan's 'Law of the Cross'. It starts off, 'Sin leads to death.' But the only death produced by sin is that of Jesus. There, and there alone, sheer life, what Rosemary Haughton calls 'exchange', sheer self-gift to the world, came up against the world in all its initial anti-life power, and this collision destroyed Jesus, drew all his blood from him. Faced with *that* death, faced with the *result* of the sin that is in me, I see my sin *as* deathwish, as that most profound turning of life against itself which only the light of Golgotha makes clear. So the *direction*, the logic of the Law, works *backwards*, from the luminous death-by-sin back to the opaque death-wish in sin itself. Lonergan states the law *forwards* from the death-wish ('Sin leads to death') to the saving death in love. Obviously, it works both ways. But it has to *be* worked both ways to become clear. 'Sin leads to death' is, necessarily, a very obscure statement. In my rewriting of the Law in Chapter 41 above, I made it *less* obscure by using my concept of sin as 'outlawing' death. But it only becomes *clear* when we reverse the law and start with the luminous death-by-sin or death-in-love, and then cast its light on sin exposing the latter as death-wish.

L. in the old days, nicknamed me 'die Schlange' (the snake). It strikes instantaneously when touched. At the same time, it *invites* touch. Jesus you are teaching me at last not to wonder why I always do this – the 'wonder why I always etc.' *is* self-downing – but to rest in that sore place. With this rest, the striking-out becomes unnecessary, the profoundest reflex of my life is changed.

I am poor with all the poverty in the world. My armoured awkwardness, de-defended, opens wide to the poor, the forgotten people of my self-securing. Only the blood of Jesus penetrates this armour. The poor only thicken it with guilt. Another interpretation of the parable of the sheep and the goats suggests itself. Jesus I *cannot* see you in my wretched brother until you face me with my own wretchedness, not my sin but my sense of being unlovable that issues in sin.

I have lived all my life in a most deep forgetfulness, of a need to be loved as myself unprotected. Protection stands between me and this memory. The story of the Fall is the story of the coming of

168

protection. Like Kipling's 'How the Elephant got its Trunk', how the human got its invisible armour.

An imposing part of my armour is the writing that draws many to God!

As I become able, in this new love of Jesus, to de-protect myself, I learn to consider my weird behaviour non-judgmentally.

J: Judge not yourself or others, rather accept your folly as my folly, so I can take you to myself, because I love you. I want you in the absolutely unqualified way a lover wants the beloved. You will not believe this, so eager are you to flee yourself.

There has been pause. God knows how – no, I know how, it is the pause of being loved by God in Jesus. 'God in Jesus' – all the linguistic mess that has come of trying to associate those names algebraically rather than mystically has cleared away. I have never before thought that *I* was all right. Never. The pre-Oedipally impelled flight from self is more insistent than the Oedipally imposed. For the Oedipal gives the child a sex and something to do with it. It covers over the not-being-all-right-to-be. And envy of the Oedipal – a very primal penis envy sharable by men – compounds the flight of the pre-Oedipal.

The madness of the pre-Oedipal flight caught up with by the madness of Jesus the man of nothing-but-love, flags me down at last.

I have never before thought that *I* was all right.

There returns the vision in the church in the Roman countryside during the singing of the anthem for Sacred Heart, 'One of the soldiers opened his side with a spear, and immediately there came out blood and water'. I saw the collision of the heart, the love-alone, with the spear, the anti-love, as the wellspring of the universe. I could see it this way because I was the heart, and I was the spear, so in me was the healing: and the *certainty* of healing is of God alone. It is the certainty that there will never be a universal order other than this in which the pierced heart is peace.

The certainty in the vision, the coming-to-rest of the never-yet-self-accepted heart in the vision, *is* the Resurrection, *is* Jesus the crucified God-empowered killed love at term. It is the Resurrection wherein I know my resting in the crucified love to be the ultimate reality of my and the world's existence.

The essence of a minimalist concept of the Resurrection is that its 'all is well' does not supervene upon a preceding 'all is ill', only upon an 'all is average'. As a pre-Oedipal, I know something about 'all is ill'. So I have something to say about the Resurrection. The 'all is well' that supervenes on 'all is ill' is of God alone. It is God raising Jesus from the dead.

More than this. The Resurrection identifies God with the pierced heart. The God so identified will judge the Church through all her Petrine compromises.

Jesus was killed by sin. But once we see this fact in a stark way and are contemplating a death that was the only possible outcome of the collision between love and unyielding unlove, then we see that death not only as *brought about* by sin but as *necessitated* by sin. And this is death not merely *by* sin but *for* sin, a death needed by sin if sin is ever to be ended or to come to any resolution. The primary insight into the Suffering Servant is precisely this: a collision of love and sin so stark that the love is seen as 'for sin' in its crucifixion which is in consequence sin's absolution. 'By his stripes we are healed.' This is the most amazing statement in the Jewish scriptures, which Voegelin sees as climaxing the revelation to Israel.

B *comments*:   This is a further step in your individuation. You have said, many times during the last few days, 'For the first time in my life . . .' There's always been an inner voice apologizing for what you're doing and how you do it. That voice had been audible to some of us at times. It must have been much more intrusive inside yourself.

In the Church today, we see a widespread attempt to create community by short-circuiting the movement into the wobble, the not-being-all-right in people. A Church built on Christ in any other way, whether by authority or by popular movement, must fail.

What about Transactional Analysis? It has its uses, but it does not have anything like the sophistication required to get to the *real* 'not feeling OK'. 'Parent, child and adult' is too compact. We are mothered and fathered, 'for God's sake!'

THE TURNING POINT

Just where I
for fear must fly
you for love
have to die.

170

Just where I
am never still
you my fear
has to kill.

Just where I
am never well
your love for me
in blood will tell.

Just where I
am never I
you 'I love you'
ever cry.

And whence this peace
of secure love?
This love is wounded
for my ease.

Such ease was never
known before
and once known
is ever more.

It offers place
to all in pain:
the wounded heart
has mine in train.

At the core
I pause, am weird:
the wounded heart
makes life unfeared.

Just where I
am panic, lost
you are I
in love, and crossed.

And just where I
am folly crushed
your folly comes
and I am rushed
to peace within
your wounded arms
wound around me –
the world calms.

Just where I
am driven most
nails are driven
in my host:

Between these two
I have to dive:
by his death
I'm caught alive.

* * * * *

Be as quiet as quiet can
while the lover operates.
Prayer is an interruption of stillness.

The bleeding body
is the one pole:
the bludgeoned self
the other.
Between these poles
love is the current.

Praying is not trying to find words;
it is words trying to find me,
it is a rhythm of the soul
that, doing itself, feels like
an attempt to find words
and partly almost is.

What is this love that overcomes the insecurity of being itself? It
comes of God overcome by my insecure violence. Embraced by this
bleeding love, I feel: 'I was never right, it was never well with me,
till now. Though I did not know it, I never felt right.'

172

The blood of my separation is flooded with the blood of love's victim. Here is a place where I would rest forever, be forever myself without desertion. This is the peace of the Resurrection, in which the victim is revealed as the self of God.

It's never been quite well with me
I now can say and love to say
to him whose loving sets me free
and turns my darkness into day.

I have heard the blood fall
in the rain forest of my memory.

His desire for me
met the spear and life cessation
whereas my desire for life
stops far short of the spear –
I find, at the heart of this foreshortening,
soreness, shame, a weird sense of self,
a weight on my back.
His desire for me, bloody,
speaks at long last to that misery
so that I hear 'I love you'
and know that it's never been quite well with me
and love to say this now
to him who lifts an infinite
imaginary burden.
Why do we carry ourselves
rather than walk ourselves?

* * * * *

I love the way you love me
tied to blood in whose dark tide
of God I feel me good as never yet
my whole life still to an evening of promise
recalled in a huge tide of never happiness:
I love the way you love me.

* * * * *

Naked in the presence of my wounded nakedness
to dare to know, you crucified,

where love is leading you inside me
is to find lovely your wounds,
their divinity, your resurrection:
through my woundedness touched
the divinity of yours.
In my dark place
your blood is light.

* * * * *

Arms about me
let me, let me hunger,
let me let be
my wound of love denied.
Only God in the flesh
can open our incest wound and enter:
blood transfusion of the crucified
love who ravishes saying 'I am you!'

* * * * *

It is not for me to say 'I am you'
until you say to me 'I am you'.

* * * * *

Surge on lover hands of skill
working like silence in my inner tangle
so that miraculously
the strands lie clear.
I do not know the work:
but I know in myself the will that it proceed.

174